MetricsMan

MetricsMan

It Doesn't Count Unless You Can Count It

Don Bartholomew

Edited by

Zifei Fay Chen

BEP BUSINESS EXPERT PRESS

MetricsMan: It Doesn't Count Unless You Can Count It

First published in 2016 by
Business Expert Press, LLC
222 East 46th Street, New York, NY 10017
www.businessexpertpress.com

ISBN-13: 978-1-63157-521-1 (paperback)
ISBN-13: 978-1-63157-522-8 (e-book)

Business Expert Press Public Relations Collection

Collection ISSN: 2157-345X (print)
Collection ISSN: 2157-3476 (electronic)

Cover and interior design by Exeter Premedia Services Private Ltd., Chennai, India

First edition: 2016

10 9 8 7 6 5 4 3 2 1

Printed in the United States of America.

Abstract

Public relations and social media research and measurement have come a long way. What are the right metrics to measure in the face of numerous tool vendors and platform choices? How can we make the results count? And how can we prove the accountability of our profession? This book presents answers to these questions from the late Don Bartholomew, the first of the *Measurati* and a great industry thought leader, through a compilation of the 67 blog posts he authored on his blog *MetricsMan* from 2006 to 2014. It entails his opinions and insights on the most important topics of public relations and social media research and measurement—the evolution of measurement over the years, return on investment (ROI), the *Barcelona Principles*, social media measurement models, marketing mix modeling (MMM), the battle against advertising value equivalents (AVEs), and the journey toward accountability. Through this book, public relations professionals will be able to set clear measurement goals and objectives, identify right from wrong in the metrics they use, and understand how to apply the valid measurement models and frameworks in their practices.

Keywords

accountability, AMEC Social Media Valid Framework, evaluation, marketing mix modeling (MMM), *Measurati*, measurement, metrics, paid-earned-shared-owned (PESO) model, public relations, return on investment (ROI), social media, the *Barcelona Principles*

Contents

Tributes to Don Bartholomew

Don was an outstanding professional who gave a lot to his firm, and he gave freely of his gifts and his time to AMEC. Without Don, who joined up with Richard Bagnall, we would not have the AMEC social media measurement framework, which is a breakthrough for our industry.

—Barry Leggetter, CEO of the International Association for the Measurement and Evaluation of Communication (AMEC)

Don was a class act and all around good egg.
You can bet he rode his bike to the pearly gates where he was met with cocktails from dear family and friends.
Don, you will be missed.
The world will have less joy (and worse grammar) without you in it.

—Michelle Hinson, Chair of the Institute for Public Relations (IPR) Measurement Commission

Don's ability to bring the analytical research world together with the digital world was a great asset and go-to source for all of us in Dallas and across the network. His dry sense of humor, passion for Syracuse basketball, and willingness to jump in on any opportunity defined him not only as a colleague, but as a friend.

—Jamey Peters, Partner/Director at Ketchum

Don gave me the chance to join the Ketchum Digital Research and Analytics team he created. I can say with 100 percent certainty that it has completely changed my career path. Thanks to him, I have soared in this environment, and without him, I truly don't know where I would be. I will be forever grateful to Don for the time he spent teaching me and helping me to become a more confident and qualified digital research and analytics professional.

—Erin Salisbury, Project Manager, Digital Research and Analytics at Ketchum

I was one of the lucky ones to get to work with Don Bartholomew, and he helped our team start a new foundation, a new definition for what measurement means for our programming. Through his guidance, he helped us see why we need the help to connect the dots. Everybody agrees that measurement is good and you need it from a philosophical standpoint. But how do you do it? How do you implement it across your teams, across your programming, and help those people who come along with you on that journey? He was one of the folks that helped to enlighten the inner measurement geek in me, which I didn't realize a few years ago that it was there, but it is strongly there now.

—Meredith Stevens, Director, Digital Strategy at National
Cattlemen's Beef Association (NCBA)

Don was a good man of great integrity whose contributions to our field were extraordinary and influenced a lot of our thinking.

—Chris Foster, Worldwide Executive Vice President,
Burson-Marsteller

Foreword

The public relations world lost a true luminary when measurement guru Don Bartholomew passed away on June 1, 2015. He had been battling brain cancer since early 2014. He is survived by his wife, Paula, and son, Seth.

Don spent the last few years at Ketchum as senior vice president for digital analytics for research and measurement. Previously, he did stints at a number of other public relations firms, including Fleishman and MWW.

He shaped measurement programs for a huge array of clients including: BMW, Gatorade, Michelin, AT&T, Novartis, Dell, Merck, and Johnson & Johnson.

He was well recognized in his field with his much-read blog *MetricsMan*. He was an *Emeritus* member of the Measurement Commission of the Institute for Public Relations, serving for many years as a dedicated professional trying to raise the profession's awareness of metrics, methodology, and evaluation.

In describing Don, Pauline Draper-Watts of Edelman Berland[1] and former IPR Commission Chair said:

> His contribution to the body of knowledge on all things measurement has left its mark; his understanding in social media has helped to shape approaches to measurement in that space and he was valued by us all, not only for his smarts but also for his humor, his smile, his company at various events and in so many other ways.

One of his most important contributions was in his role as vice chair of AMEC's Social Media Measurement Group. In that capacity, he and

---

[1] Editor: Edelman Berland is now known as Edelman Intelligence.

Richard Bagnall of Prime Research wrote what has become the industry's standard for social media measurement.

At the 2015 AMEC Summit in Stockholm, two days after Don passed away, one of his students of measurement—Meredith Stevens of NCBA—presented the adaptation of his work to the U.S. beef industry. "We would not be here today if it weren't for Don's leadership and good counsel," she said.

Don and I were buddies for probably a dozen years before we started working together, so, while he reported to me as part of the Ketchum Global Research and Analytics team, I mainly thought of him as a friend. Frankly, as an employee, he could be a bit of a pain—often questioning things I had decided, and even worse, usually being right. The impact he had on our organization will be remembered for years to come—and his influence on the memories of those who had the pleasure to work with him will last a lifetime.

David Rockland, PhD
Partner/CEO
Ketchum Global Research and Analytics

Introduction

Public relations research and measurement has come a long way. Accountability of the profession is not gained overnight. To get the metrics right and make the results count, a long journey has been made by the *Measurati* (Burke 2015) who constantly seek to improve the measurement standards.

The first of the *Measurati* and a thought leader in public relations research and measurement (The Measurement Standard 2015), Mr. Don Bartholomew had left us the legacy of his own journey through his influential blog *MetricsMan*. This book picks up the legacy to honor him with a compilation of 67 blog posts authored by Don from 2006 to 2014. A must-read for all public relations professionals, *MetricsMan* presents Don's opinions and insights on the most important topics of public relations and social media research and measurement—return on investment (ROI), the *Barcelona Principles*, social media measurement models, and the marketing mix modeling (MMM), to name a few.

In this book, the 67 blog posts are categorized into eight different chapters, each featuring an important theme of public relations measurement.

Chapter 1 "The Coming of Age of Measurement" presents the evolution of public relations measurement over the years and provides an outlook for the future. In his blog posts, Don pointed out the damages brought by the inappropriately used metrics such as outputs, impressions, and advertising value equivalents (AVEs). To advocate the value of public relations and social media programs, he proposed some new and more valid metrics for measurement such as the exposure–engagement–influence–impact–advocacy model and the PESO (Paid, Earned, Shared, and Owned media) spectrum.

ROI is perhaps one of the most discussed, yet agonized-over, topics in public relations and social media measurement. **Chapter 2 "Demystifying Return on Investment"** clarifies the definition and metrics, and introduces the framework and research approaches for social media ROI measurement. Some blog posts included in this chapter also feature the debates on the application of MMM and the possible (but wrong) use of multipliers.

Chapter 3 "'Puzzles' Versus 'Pieces'—Getting the Metrics Right" further elucidates the right and wrong metrics used in public relations and social media measurement. The blog posts included in this chapter address the question: Are we solving the actual "puzzles" or are we merely calculating the "pieces" in the metrics we adopted? To better solve the real "puzzles," Don introduced the International Association for the Measurement and Evaluation of Communication (AMEC) *Social Media Valid Framework* and explained how it could be used in social media measurement.

Social media continues to gain momentum in the measurement sphere and better knowledge is called for facing the explosion of social media tool vendors and platform choices. As a great portion of blog posts on *MetricsMan* are related to social media measurement, **Chapter 4 "The 'Tail' and the 'Dog' in Social Media Measurement"** and **Chapter 5 "Getting a Robust and Effective Social Media Measurement Program"** are specifically devoted to this topic. While it can get technical in choosing the tools (the "tail"), the measurement objectives, stakeholders, and correct metrics (the "dog") should always come first. These two chapters also include a series of posts on the plan–select–deploy process to choose social media measurement tools as well as the social media listening maturity model for professionals and organizations to evaluate their practices against.

Chapter 6 "The Deadly Sins of Advertising Value Equivalents" showcases Don's long-time battle against AVEs. The once overused AVEs equate public relations to media relations and do not measure outcome. To fight against the wrong metrics, a list of 12 "deadly sins" of AVEs is presented, based on the collaborated efforts made by Don and other public relations measurement thought leaders. The wrongdoings of AVEs are also further depicted in examples.

Chapter 7 "Thus Spoke the *Measurati*"[2] highlights some of the most heated topics in public relations research and measurement. This chapter not only presents Don's own opinions, but also thoughts from many other thought leaders featured in his blog articles. For example, insights from Barry Leggetter, Pauline Draper-Watts, and Dr. David Rockland are presented in a blog post on the *Barcelona Principles*. This chapter also highlights a fascinating and important debate over relationship measurement. Comments to Don's post made by Katie Paine, Todd Defren, Dr. James Grunig, and Mark Weiner were also included. While the correct answer is beyond the scope of this book, readers are encouraged to contemplate after being exposed to both sides of the argument.

Chapter 8 "Gaining Accountability—Making It Count" concludes the book with a compilation of the blog posts focusing on *accountability*. For the public relations profession to gain a seat at the management table, accountability is no longer optional. To prove the profession's accountability, Don provided a public relations value cube and pointed out that the value of public relations lies in the scope of measurement.

In 2015, the Ketchum Excellence in Public Relations Research Award sponsored by Ketchum Global Research and Analytics (KGRA) and Institute for Public Relations (IPR) was renamed after Mr. Don Bartholomew to honor his leadership in public relations and his passion for teaching others the best practices of research and measurement. As recipient of the inaugural *Don Bartholomew Award for Excellence in Public Relations Research* sponsored by Ketchum and IPR, I feel extremely honored. More

---

[2] Barry Leggetter is the CEO of AMEC. Pauline Draper-Watts is Executive Vice President of Edelman Intelligence's US Communications and Measurement Analytics group. David Rockland, PhD, is partner/CEO of Ketchum Global Research and Analytics and past chairman of AMEC. Katie Paine, "The Measurement Queen," is the CEO of Paine Publishing. Todd Defren is CEO of SHIFT Communication. James Grunig, PhD, is Professor *Emeritus* at the University of Maryland. Mark Weiner is CEO of PRIME Research.

importantly, I feel the urge to learn more about Don's great contributions and the responsibility to carry on his legacy through research and practice. I did not get the chance to meet Don in person—I really wish I had. However, during the two months of my fellowship at KGRA, I felt that Don was still there, through the models and metrics he provided that are being applied in our work, and through his philosophy of measurement that is being inherited here and in the public relations industry.

Reading through *MetricsMan* while editing this book, I could feel having conversations with Don. I could feel his passion for measurement and his eagerness to improve the accountability of our profession. "It doesn't count unless you can count it"—as the title of this book implies, the accountability and the future of the public relations profession resides in the way it is measured. Learning from the legacy Don left us and making our own efforts to help advance the public relations profession is perhaps the best way to honor our Godfather of the *Measurati*.

CHAPTER 1

The Coming of Age of Measurement

Don pushed our thinking. That's what he was good at. He built the next step in thinking that allowed/forced the next person to up their thinking and come up with the next step up the staircase. His MetricsMan blog, from April 2006 to June 2014, was always reasoned, sane, and without hyperbole. It was well written and well argued. Many times, the thinking was original, with ideas that made the reader say "I never thought of that." It didn't matter if you agreed or not, his blog post always made you think. What made Don great was both the soundness of his thinking and the fact that he put that thinking out there in the public sphere for all to critique.

—Fraser Likely, President of Likely Communications
Strategies Ltd.

This chapter includes:

- What we did wrong in the past for public relations research and measurement
- The right metrics for measurement
- The exposure–engagement–influence–impact–advocacy model, the PESO (paid, earned, shared, and owned) spectrum and their applications
- How to integrate data and insights
- Trends and outlook of public relations measurement

Five Public Relations Measurement Trends
to Watch in 2008

(January 16, 2008)

Look for 2008 to be a year of increasing accountability for the public relations profession. Add in the very real possibility of an economic recession and, more than ever, the pressure will be on to prove the value of public relations.

1. **Focus on efforts to measure the influence of blogs, social media, and other online properties**

    There is a high level of agreement that blogs, discussion groups, social media, and other online properties are shaping the way consumers learn and think about products and brands. First-generation attempts to measure their influence on consumers have been done using predominately traditional media metrics such as impressions.[1] In 2008 expect to see a stronger push toward specialized metrics to measure online engagement/dialog rather than just exposure.

2. **Ongoing shift of public relations measurement budgets toward Outcomes rather than Outputs**

    Historically, the majority of public relations dollars have been spent on measuring Outputs (Exposure) rather than Outcomes (Influence and Action). Studies suggest that the split has been perhaps 60/40 percent. We expect 2008 to be the first year where the split is closer to 50/50 percent.

3. **Renewed efforts by content providers to reconcile copyright issues**

    Many of you may have recently received a letter from BurrellesLuce (BurrellesLuce, 2008) notifying you as of April 2008, they will be adding copyright royalty fees automatically on behalf of content owners based on the average numbers of copies of print or electronic

---

[1] Editor: an impression is "a metric that indicates the number of possible exposures of a media item to a defined set of stakeholders; the number of people who might have had the opportunity to be exposed to a story that has appeared in the media" (Stacks and Bowen 2013, 11).

clips distributed. Expect other content aggregators to follow suit in 2008.

4. **Increased use of marketing mix modeling (MMM) for return on investment (ROI) determination**

   Procter and Gamble's proactive outreach about their MMM project (*More information in article "ROI—Is statistical modeling the answer? Depends on the question" in Chapter 2*) sparked a lot of industry debate in 2007 (and we suspect projects for modeling vendors). The new Da Vinci agency being formed for Dell has already stated that their ambition is to combine art and science to tie marketing activities directly to business outcomes such as sales and market share. Look for MMM to be part of the science used by Da Vinci and for it to become mainstreamed in 2008.

5. **Additional efforts to find a "single metric" measurement solution**

   For many in public relations measurement, the Holy Grail is a single, powerful metric of success. Microsoft took this approach with their ambitious measurement system development project last year as did the Canadian Public Relations Society (*More information in article "Oh, Canada—Is MRP the Answer?" in Chapter 2*) before them. Perhaps Da Vinci will also be seduced by the allure of the single metric.

The Future State of Public Relations Measurement—2013

(September 8, 2008)

I believe it was Neils Bohr, or perhaps Yogi Berra, who once said, "Predictions are difficult, especially about the future." In 2008, the public relations industry is undergoing rapid change driven by Web 2.0 phenomenon such as social media, blogging, peer-to-peer communications, and synchronous communications. As the influence of traditional media diminishes due to ongoing fragmentation, public relations firms are re-inventing themselves to help clients navigate and succeed in this new reality.

Here are a few predictions for the future state of public relations measurement. I almost guarantee that these will be wrong.

More than half of all measurement dollars go to Outcomes research rather than (just) measuring Outputs. Historically, the majority of public relations measurement dollars have gone toward Outputs (exposure) rather than Outcomes (influence and action). For most major public relations programs, it is no longer considered sufficient to just measure Outputs. Clients and companies increasingly demand to understand what actually happened as a result of getting a media hit rather than celebrating just getting the hit.

Cross-platform/domain measurement of a hot topic. How do you measure the influence on someone who has read your blog, posted a comment, sent a tweet to 35 followers, visited another site and referred to your blog with a trackback, told four friends about your post, two of whom visited your blog as well? Communication tools such as advertising and public relations have always worked together synergistically. By 2013, the number of ways of interacting and participating in communities of interest would have greatly complicated the measurement task.

Word-of-Mouth (WOM) measurement will be another of the hot topics. While both public relations and advertising claim that they are the rightful "owners" of WOM programs, neither is able to offer a comprehensive way to assign a value to a peer-to-peer conversation or recommendation. By the way, it is nonsensical to try to use ad value equivalents (AVEs) for WOM. It makes even less sense than using AVEs for earned print media.

Marketing mix modeling (MMM) is mainstream. In response to cross-platform measurement challenges, an increase in interest in integrated marketing communication, and a continuing need to demonstrate accountability, MMM will be commonly used in 2013 to report on the efficacy of large programs containing multiple communications tactics (advertising, public relations, public affairs, direct, etc.).

Industry proliferation and consolidation. The public relations measurement industry is undergoing a proliferation of vendors in 2008. For example, the number of social media measurement firms roughly doubled from 50 in 2007 to 100 in 2008. Beginning in 2009 and continuing through 2013, there will be a series of company failures and consolidations that would leave about five large, strong measurement firms and a second tier of perhaps 20 specialist firms.

There will be a variety of free or very low cost public relations measurement tools. These will become available online and will make it very easy to obtain good Output data at low or no cost.

There will still be no standard metric for public relations measurement. Despite many efforts, there will be no agreement on a single, standard metric for public relations measurement. Objectives vary widely and metrics need to reflect this. In the social media space, Nielsen (n.d.) Buzz-Metrics will be considered a de facto standard by many practitioners.

We will still be talking about AVEs. The continuing quest for accountability and ROI will cause many to follow the easy and misguided route of AVEs. This despite the fact that numerous professional organizations, including PRSA and the IPR,[2] have come out against the further use of AVEs in the industry.

Five Social Media and Public Relations Measurement Trends to Watch in 2009

(January 8, 2009)

As we launch into a year with perhaps as much uncertainty, on multiple levels, as most of us have known, I offer my fearless predictions for 2009. The single most interesting dynamic this year in my view is the tension between an increasing need for accountability and tight budgets.

1. **Social media dominates measurement conversation**

   In June 2008, I did a quick blog analysis to understand the volume of posts about public relations/public relations measurement compared to social media measurement. About 80 percent of all posts were specific to social media measurement. I repeated the analysis for December 2008 and got the same result. Social media measurement is dominating the conversation. It is interesting to note that the social media measurement online conversation is not being driven (with a couple of notable exceptions) by the firms and individuals associated with traditional *media content analysis*. They seem to be followers and

---

[2] Editor: PRSA—Public Relations Society of America; IPR—Institute for Public Relations.

not leaders. New players and voices are emerging, particularly from the web analytics world.

2. **Quest for standards**

For many in public relations measurement, the Holy Grail is a single, powerful metric of success. A standard metric, which everyone generally agrees with and can be applied consistently, would enable lowering of costs, leading to greater measurement participation, and allow agencies and companies to compete on actual results, that is, audience effects, not on cutesy proprietary metrics and algorithms. Or so the argument goes. In the other camp are the "snowflake measurement" disciples who say that each public relations program and set of objectives is unique and therefore requires unique measurement approaches—standardization doesn't apply to snowflakes. Driven by a desire to find "standard" social media metrics, look for the standardization argument to be a hot topic again in 2009.

3. **Engagement will be the hot social media metric**

Many have said that Web 2.0 is about "engagement and not eyeballs." Indeed, it looks like Engagement will be the metric of the moment in 2009. While everyone might agree, at a macro level, that Engagement is about the engagement between individuals and brands, there is almost no agreement on what Engagement really means, particularly in the online world. There are many different views at different levels of abstraction:

- *BusinessWeek* has a Reader Engagement Index that they calculate as comments to posts ratio. An Engagement Index of 5 would indicate 5 comments per post.
- Forrester Research defines the engagement between individuals and brands in terms of the four Is: Involvement, Interaction, Intimacy, and Influence.
- And, well-known web analytics guru Eric T. Peterson has developed an eight-term equation for Engagement that includes clicks, recency, duration, brand, feedback, interaction, loyalty, and subscriptions.

Look for many other definitions and points of view on Engagement in 2009. Measuring Community and Velocity may also be hot social media metrics.

4. Cross-platform/Domain measurement challenges

How do you measure the influence on someone who has read your blog, posted a comment, sent a tweet to 35 followers, visited another site, referred to your blog with a trackback, texted four friends about your post, two of whom visited your blog as well? Most measurement approaches and tools today are tied to specific platforms and not to people. As communication increasingly becomes horizontal/ peer-to-peer—online and offline—our ability to measure discrete programs becomes exponentially more difficult. It would seem that a greater emphasis on holistic approaches that are audience-centric might be a partial solution. Look for measurement firms to begin addressing this challenge in 2009.

5. A battle of good (accountability) versus evil (economy)

So far, the spirit of experimentation in social media has provided a sort of "get out of jail free" card with respect to having to demonstrate the value of digital and social media programs and initiatives. It looks like all that could change, as 2009 will be primarily driven by the economic climate. In 2009, the pendulum will swing from experimentation to accountability. This year will raise the bar on all of us to demonstrate how social media and other public relations programs are helping to drive desired business outcomes. Acting against this pendulum swing are the Evils of flat or reduced 2009 budgets. It will be easy for many people facing budget pressures to reduce or eliminate measurement. But you do this at the peril of credible accountability. What do you think will win in 2009—Good or Evil?

Public Relations Measurement 2010: Five Things to Forget and Five Things to Learn

(July 29, 2009)

Public relations measurement is at a crossroads. Old techniques are no longer sufficient. Old metrics are no longer applicable. Old thinking must be replaced by new. The need for accountability, and to prove the value of public relations and social media programs, has never been greater.

As we look to the next year, here are five things to forget and five things to learn about public relations measurement in 2010.

Things to Forget in 2010

1. *Media relations focus*

   A focus on media relations fails to capture several important aspects of public relations—brand, reputation, crisis, employee communication, and direct-to-consumer advertising (DTC), to name a few. Also, the importance of traditional media is declining. Numerous studies have shown that people don't trust what they read in the media. They trust each other. I believe it was Hauser and Katz who coined the term "you are what you measure" in 1998. If measurement is focused on media relations, then that is how the public relations function will be judged.

2. *Outputs*

   The need to put public relations results in a business context has never been greater. We need to be able to address the question—"What are we doing to help drive the business?" If you are focused on output metrics like impressions or message delivery, you will always have a hard time explaining business impact. Instead, we need to focus on outcomes and answer the question—what happened as a result of our program or coverage? Understanding outputs has primary benefit as a diagnostic tool rather than a "scorecard."

3. *Impressions (and Multipliers!)*

   The most common public relations metric today is Impressions. While it is a somewhat dubious metric for traditional media, it really loses meaning in social media where engagement, not eyeballs, is what we seek. Impressions also (greatly) overstate actual relevant audience. Generally, only a fraction of any particular magazine or newspaper's circulation meets your target audience demographics. And impressions merely represent an opportunity to see; they do not attempt to estimate the (small) percentage of the potential audience that actually saw your content. To compound the problems, many public relations professionals use a multiplier on impression numbers to account for pass-along readership or a mythical credibility advantage public relations has over other communication tools. The simple fact is there is no factual basis (e.g., research proof) for using multipliers in any case.

4. *Ad equivalency (AVEs)*

There are many reasons why using ad equivalency as a proxy for public relations value is not advisable. Here are five good reasons they should be avoided:

- AVE calculations vary and there are no standards. Tonality, article length, competitive mentions, and other factors are handled differently.
- AVE results can be misleading. AVEs may be trending up while metrics such as message communication, share of favorable positioning, and share of positive press are falling.
- AVEs reduce public relations to just the media dimension by only assigning a value in this area.
- AVEs only apply to traditional media. What is the AVE of a positive conversation about your company on a leading blog?
- How much is it worth for a troubled company to not appear in the *Wall Street Journal?* AVEs cannot address this.

5. *Return on (engagement/influence/etc.)*

Not a day goes by on Twitter without someone declaring a new and improved metric for the acronym ROI, or stating that ROI does not apply in social networks. Wrong and wrong. Most of these folks either don't understand ROI or don't know how to obtain the data necessary to calculate it. There is also a lot of confusion between creating value and ROI. Generating awareness creates value, for example, but may not immediately result in demonstrable ROI.[3]

Things to Learn in 2010

1. *Total value of public relations*

The majority of current public relations measurement efforts focus on marketing/sales and output metrics. The total value cube (Figure 1.1) is a way to visualize and think about all the potential value your public relations and social media efforts deliver. Beyond marketing to include brand and reputation, beyond outputs to

---

[3] Editor: See Chapter 2 for more on this discussion.

include engagement, influence, and action, and beyond revenue generation to include cost savings and cost avoidance.

2. *A new model for measurement*

Many public relations professionals regularly get their Outputs confused with their Outtakes or Outcomes. Outtakes is not often used in the United States—it seems much more prevalent in Europe. The overall terminology is confusing and is defined in different ways by different professionals. Further compounding the confusion is the fact that the audiences we present our results to rarely understand the terms and have trouble relating to them. In short, the terms are too much "inside baseball."

What we need is a metrics taxonomy that is easier to understand and explain. I like this one (Figure 1.2).

- *Exposure*—to what degree have we created exposure to content and message?
- *Engagement*—who, how, and where are people interacting/engaging with our content?

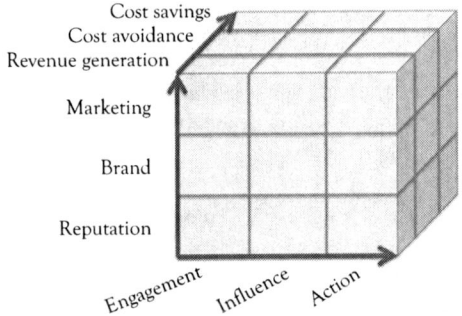

Figure 1.1 *Public relations value cube*

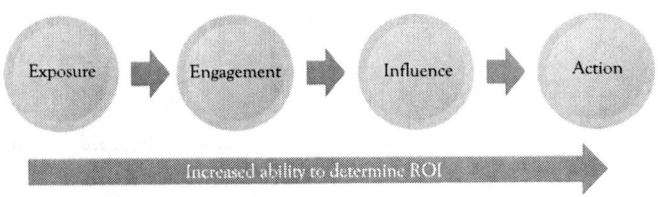

Figure 1.2 *Exposure–engagement–influence–action model*

- *Influence*—the degree to which exposure and engagement have influenced perceptions and attitudes.
- *Action*—as a result of the public relations/social media effort, what actions if any has the target taken?

3. *Three zones of measurement*

As shown in Figure 1.3, from the left, companies or brands control, own, or manage websites—corporate sites, Facebook pages, Twitter accounts, LinkedIn pages, and blogs by way of example—and create content that consumers may engage with. This zone is measured primarily by *web analytics.*[4] In the middle are the actual social networks and conversations between individuals. In this zone, we are interested in data sets that cannot be gathered solely using web analytics packages. How often is the brand being mentioned in conversation? What is the sentiment of the comments? How often is the brand being recommended and by whom? Content and behavior analyses, including tracking technologies, are the primary measurement tools in this zone. The third zone represents all the real-world, offline transactions that may be of interest. Did someone visit the store or attend or event? Did they buy a product? Did they recommend the brand or product to a friend over coffee? Primary audience research is necessary to address many of the questions, as well as scan or other purchase data in some cases.

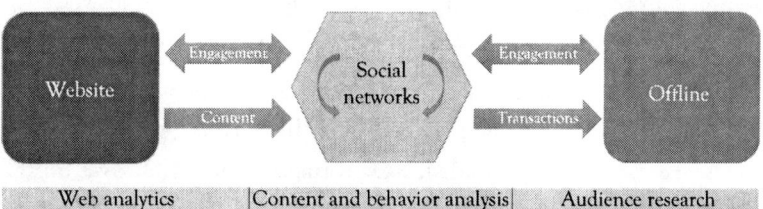

Figure 1.3 Zones of measurement

---

[4] Editor: web analytics refer to "the measurement, collection, analysis, and reporting of Internet data for purposes of understanding and optimizing web usage" (Stacks and Bowen 2013, 34).

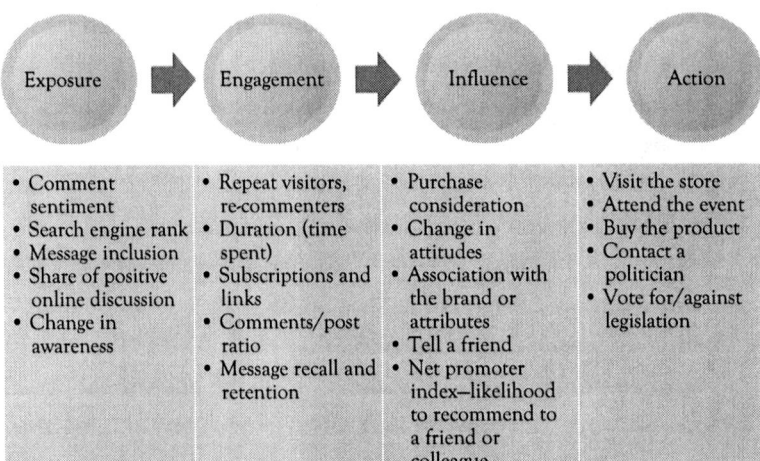

Figure 1.4 Exposure–engagement–influence–action model

Your measurement strategy should be to take a holistic, integrated approach using methodologies, tools, and data from all three zones. The Holy Grail in many ways is to be able to track behavior of individuals across all three zones, cross-platform, understanding how online behavior impacts offline behavior and vice versa.

4. *New metrics*

The new metrics might look much like what I have argued in Figure 1.4.

5. *The difference between impact/value and ROI*

ROI is a form of value/impact, but not all value takes the form of ROI. ROI is a financial metric—percentage of dollars returned for a given investment/cost. The dollars may be revenue generated, dollars saved, or spending avoided. ROI is transactional. ROI lives on the income statement in business terms.

Value is created when people become aware of us, engage with our content or brand ambassadors, are influenced by this engagement, and take some action such as recommending to a friend or buying our product. Value creation occurs over time, not at a point in time. Value creation is process-oriented. Value lives on the balance sheet.

Your investments in social media or public relations remain an investment, creating additional value if done correctly, until which time they can be linked to a business outcome transaction that results in ROI.

The Digitization of Research and Measurement

(May 12, 2010)

The field of public relations has undergone two major revolutions in the past 15 years or so. The advent of the Internet represents the first revolution. This revolution primarily impacted the way content was created, distributed, and consumed. It also fundamentally changed the nature of communication—remember e-mail became the first killer app of the Internet revolution. The second revolution is social networks. Again, content creation was impacted, led by consumer-generated content in multiple forms. Perhaps more importantly, peer-to-peer communication between consumers, and two-way communication between consumers and brands/companies, have been enabled and are having a profound impact on the way companies are organized and behave. The worlds of marketing and public relations have made an analog-to-digital conversion. And with it, we are in the midst of the digitization research and measurement.

New Models, New Metrics

Communication models are a linear representation of how a communication process works and are important in providing a framework for evaluation and measurement. The Outputs→Outtakes→Outcomes communication model often used in public relations today has two primary deficiencies in the era of digitization and social networks—clarity and relevance.

- *Clarity*: The model is difficult for many to understand and apply. Public relations professionals regularly get Outputs confused with Outtakes or Outcomes. Outtakes are not often used in the United States—they seem much more prevalent in Europe. The overall taxonomy can be confusing and is defined in different ways by different professionals or organizations. Further compounding the confusion is the fact that the audiences we present our results to, rarely understand the terms and have trouble relating to them. In short, the terms are too much "inside baseball."

- *Relevance*: The model was developed when communication was media-centric. Digitization, consumer-generated content, and social networks have shifted communication from a media-centric world to a content-centric world. How receivers of communication engage and are influenced by content has fundamentally changed.

What is needed is a metrics taxonomy that is easier to explain, understand, and apply; ideally, one that is applicable for traditional and social media. Figure 1.5 presents the model we applied at Fleishman–Hillard.

With the new model comes new metrics primarily driven by social media/networks. Exposure includes traditional metrics such as Impressions and Message Delivery, and digital metrics such as Search Rank, Twitter Reach, and Average Daily Visitors. Engagement includes traditional metrics such as Readership, but adds new metrics such as Subscriptions, Repeat Visitors, and Follower Mention percentage. *Influence* in the model refers to influence of the target audience, not who has influence in social networks. Influence metrics range from increases in Brand Consideration to changes in attitudes and opinions to changes in online click behavior. Action metrics can range from event attendance to voting for/against legislation to buying a product.

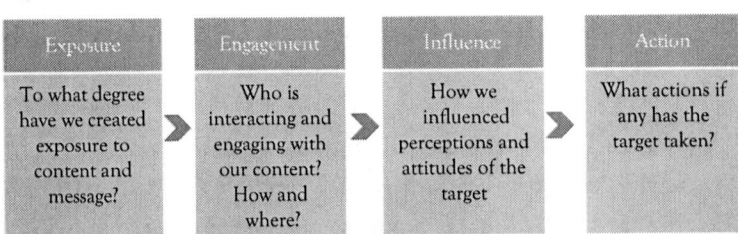

Figure 1.5 Exposure–engagement–influence–action model

Note: Used with Permission of Fleishman–Hillard.

New Data, New Places

Public relations research and measurement has historically been driven by content analysis. As content increasingly became available in digital form, the techniques of research and measurement didn't change so much as the way content was aggregated and delivered for analysis. Then web-based platforms became available from a variety of vendors to digitize and automate content analysis, while the metrics being measured—article counts, impressions, message uptake, and sentiment for example—primarily remained constant with previous, more manual methods. Today, the digitization of research and measurement has broadened from this predominately singular focus to include data and interactions from three distinct regions or zones of research and measurement as shown in Figure 1.6.

As company websites, e-Commerce sites, and other forms of "owned" media proliferated, web analytics software provided an explosion of data and new metrics such as unique visitors, page views, click-through rates, duration; referring sites and conversions became widely used and reported. We became over-served with data and underserved with insight.

The exponential rise in the popularity of social networks in the last five years raised the bar again and presented new challenges in digital research and measurement. Now we were faced with measuring conversations and not just clicks. Measuring engagement became more important than measuring eyeballs. The frontier in social media measurement is evolving toward measuring both the conversations and behavior patterns occurring within social networks, and understanding and connecting the underlying influences and motivations for the online behavior.

The third area of interest is in all the real-world, offline interactions and transactions. Scan and other digital sales data is important for

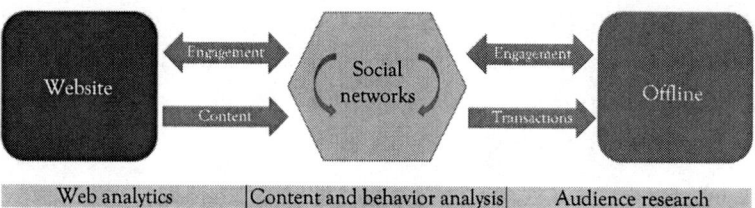

Figure 1.6 The new research and measurement model

understanding, tracking, and connecting online and offline behavior and actions. Connecting mobile transactions, online and offline behavior, and word-of-mouth (WOM) is a significant challenge.

Although we have attempted to define three distinct "zones" of digital research and measurement necessary to address the full spectrum of social media and marketing impact, a robust measurement strategy should take a holistic, integrated approach using methodologies, tools, data, and metrics from all three zones. The goal is to be able to track the behavior, interactions, and transactions of individuals across all three zones, multiple platforms, and physical locations, and to understand how online behavior impacts offline behavior and vice versa.

New Scope, New Integration

Today at Fleishman–Hillard, we recognize that the very definition of public relations is rapidly evolving to encompass a much broader and more integrated view of communications and how we connect, engage, and build relationships with consumers and other stakeholders on behalf of our clients. Digitization in all its forms has driven and accelerated this important change. While public relations has traditionally been oriented toward "earned media"—gaining placements of client stories in print and broadcast media based on the strength of the story and quality of the pitch—today's content-driven world demands much more. The scope now must include all the consumer touch points available in our increasingly digital world. We capture this new scope and integration in a model we refer to as PESO—paid/earned/shared/owned. Our PESO model predates the similar Forrester model (paid/earned/owned) and is different in an important way. We created two categories, earned and shared, whereas the other model has only one—earned. We believe that this categorization better comprehends strategies such as blogger outreach and other proactive efforts undertaken by professionals as "Earned," which is distinct from efforts that may be passive or reactive. Here is how we define the elements of our model:

- *Paid*—refers to all forms of paid content that exists on third-party channels or venues. This includes banner or display advertisements, pay-per-click programs, sponsorships, and advertorials.

- *Earned*—includes traditional media outreach as well as blogger relations/outreach where we attempt to influence and encourage third-party content providers to write about our clients and their products and services.
- *Shared*—refers to social networks and technologies controlled by consumers along with online and offline WOM.
- *Owned*—includes all websites and web properties controlled by a company or brand, including company or product websites, micro-sites, blogs, Facebook pages, and Twitter channels.

The enhanced scope and integration represented by the PESO model drives a corresponding broadening need for integration in digital research and measurement. Professionals can easily find themselves attempting to measure a highly integrated program that includes the awareness created with paid media, the relevance and information delivered via owned media, the credibility delivered by earned media, and measuring the conversations and interactions occurring in shared media. Just from a metrics perspective, the PESO model requires a significant broadening in thinking as shown in Table 1.1.

Digitization has changed what we need to research and measure, where we find data, and how we perform analysis. The future will bring more data, better tools, and improved methodologies. Sifting insights from the mounds of data will remain a major challenge. The intersection of marketing, privacy concerns, and research must be navigated. The constant in all the change brought by digitization is *who*—human analysts and research. Discovery and insight, as it was 15 years ago, remains fundamentally a human process. It remains the analog constant in a world of digitization.

Measurement 2020 and Other Fantasies

(September 23, 2011)

At the 3rd European Summit on Measurement held in Lisbon in June 2011, standardization, education, ROI, and measurement ubiquity

Table 1.1 *PESO and exposure–engagement–influence–action matrix*

	EXPOSURE	ENGAGEMENT	INFLUENCE	ACTION
Paid	• Opportunities to see • Impressions • Click-throughs • TRPs	• Interaction rate • Duration (time spent) • Branded search • Cost per click	• Purchase consideration • Change in opinion or attitudes • Association with key brand attributes	• Visit website • Attend the event • Buy the product • Play the game/contest • Download a coupon
Earned	• Comment sentiment • Organic search rank • Message inclusion • Impressions • Net positive impressions	• Readership • Message recall and retention • Awareness • Call center calls • URL visits	• Purchase consideration • Change in opinion or attitudes • Association with key brand attitudes	• Visit the store • Attend the event • Buy the product • Vote for/against
Shared	• Branded mentions • Share of positive online discussion • Comment sentiment • Number of followers, likes	• Comments/post ratio • Number of links • Number of re-tweets • Bookmarks/votes/likes • Resolution rate	• Tell a friend • Likelihood to recommend to a friend • Ratings • Reviews	• Visit the store • Attend the event • Buy the product • Vote for/against
Owned	• Unique visitors, cost per unique visitor • Page views • Click-throughs • Search rank	• Return visits • Interaction rate • Re-commenters • Duration (time spent) • Subscriptions	• Tell a friend • Change in opinion or attitudes • Association with key brand attributes	• Download white paper • Download game or app • Buy the product • Request more info

Note: Used with permission of Fleishman–Hillard.

emerged as the key themes in response to a call to set the Measurement Agenda 2020. Delegates to the conference voted on 12 priorities they thought were most important to focus on in the period leading up to 2020. The top four vote-getters became the Measurement Agenda 2020:

- How to measure the ROI of public relations (89 percent).
- Create and adopt global standards for social media measurement (83 percent).
- Measurement of public relations campaigns and programs needs to become an intrinsic part of the public relations toolkit (73 percent).
- Institute a client education program such that clients insist on measurement of outputs, outcomes, and business results from public relations programs (61 percent).

A very nice overview of the Lisbon session and the Barcelona Principles that came before is available from the post by Dr. David Rockland of Ketchum who chaired the Barcelona and Lisbon sessions (Rockland 2011). David pretty much said it all on these sessions, so I'll just add a couple of comments and share a few thoughts on what I believe the future of measurement 2020 could be.

The rallying cry coming out of Barcelona has been focused and loud—death to AVEs! Will there be a similar thematic coming out of Lisbon and what might it be? My money is on *standardization*, borne out of cross-industry cooperation. As David points out in his post, and in the words of the Chairman of International Association for the Measurement and Evaluation of Communication (AMEC) Mike Daniels, "The Summit identified some significant challenges for the public relations profession to address by 2020. However, what we also accomplished in Lisbon beyond setting the priorities was to harness the commitment and energy of the industry to agree what we need to do together" (Institute for Public Relations 2011). The current cooperation and collaboration between industry groups—AMEC, IPR, PRSA, and the Council of Public Relations Firms—is unprecedented in my time in this industry and is focused on tangible outcomes. Cross-organization committees are already at work, developing standard metrics for social media measurement, for example. The spirit of cooperation is uplifting. While the outward thematic appears to be standardization, cooperation is the enabling force.

I was also struck by the symmetry of the call to end AVEs in Barcelona and the call to codify ways to measure ROI in Lisbon. One follows the other. In my opinion, the primary reason AVEs exist is because public relations professionals feel pressured to prove the value of what they do, and quite often they are asked to describe the impact in financial terms. AVEs are perceived as a path of least resistance to express financial value. Except, as we all know, AVEs don't really have anything to do with the impact public relations creates. They are a misguided proxy for financial value, hence the need for research-based methods to determine true ROI.

All the priorities coming out of Lisbon are excellent goals for the industry. And similar to David Rockland, I believe that they will be achieved, and be achieved before 2020. Here are three other items on my wish list for Measurement 2020:

> *Word of mouth/Word of mouse integration*: For those of us focused in social media and other digital technologies, we can't allow our digital lens to color what is fundamentally an analog world. Research studies suggest the majority of word of mouth (WOM) happens in real life. From an influence perspective, I don't think too many would argue that word of mouth from a trusted friend or family member is more powerful than word of mouth from someone you follow on Twitter. Digital cross-platform research is difficult enough, but when one huge platform is "real life," we have significant challenges in measurement. WOMMA[5] and others have made early attempts to define measurement approaches for offline WOM, but much work remains. We need ways to assess its impact and then we need to think about ways to attribute value to that impact. Mobile is a wildcard here, as it becomes the preferred platform for online activity. The need to triangulate online, mobile,

---

[5] Word of Mouth Marketing Association. http://womma.org/

and "real life" measurement presents significant challenges today, and may still by 2020.

Cookie wars: We all know the measurement versus privacy showdown is coming, right? The first shots have already been fired. The collection of source-level personal data, enabled by cookies, is crucial to measurement and insights but has the potential for misuse or unintended disclosure. Some sophisticated consumers have had their fill of cookies. Although the broader issue might be framed as social sharing versus privacy control, how it plays out will have a direct impact on digital analytics and measurement.

Integrated measurement across the paid-earned-shared-owned (PESO) spectrum: Measurement has increasingly become integrated. It began with integrated traditional (earned) and social media (shared) measurement and then progressed rapidly to earned, owned, and shared, which is where most integrated measurement programs are today. Many leading edge integrated programs today also include advertising or paid media. By 2020, integrated measurement across the PESO spectrum will most likely be the norm and not the exception. A key enabling element here in my view is some base level of agreement on how each area should be measured and standard metrics for each. It will take significant cooperation between industry groups, vendors, agencies, and major customers/clients for cross-discipline standardization to move forward effectively. We are at the beginning of this movement in 2011. By 2020, it will be fascinating to look back and see how all this plays out.

When looking ahead to 2020, I am reminded of a measurement discussion pulled together by *PRWeek* a couple of years ago. Many of the *Measurati* attended. In response to a question of where measurement will be in five years, David Rockland replied (paraphrasing here), "Who knows? Five years ago who would have guessed we would all be focused on how to measure social media?" So, there is a certain fantasy element to discussing 2020 challenges in measurement (Figure 1.7). What are your measurement fantasies?

Figure 1.7 2020 challenge?

Digital Analytics—From Back Office to Front Page

(March 21, 2013)

Analytics have exploded into prominence in the past 15 months. What was once a mysterious statistical discipline understood by few has been elevated as *the* enabling technology that allows companies to unlock the potential of "Big Data." Big Data was everywhere in 2012. There was a track devoted to it at the World Economic Forum in January 2012. In October, the *Harvard Business Review* had a cover section on Big Data, which characterized analytics as sexy and dubbed its leading practitioners Data Scientists. And at Ketchum, we made analytics training mandatory for ALL employees in 2012, a first for our industry.

The digitization of all forms of analog data is at the heart of the Big Data explosion. From our click behavior online to purchases we make with a loyalty card to places we go in our vehicles, everything is captured as digital data potentially available for analysis. And with the accelerating use of cameras and sensors, the volume of data promises to keep rising for years to come.

For all the talk about Big Data, no one really wants Big Data. They want the insights hidden within the data that only digital analytics can unlock. Probably the hottest area within digital analytics is *predictive analytics.* Predictive analytics essentially predict how consumers will behave given certain conditions, assumptions, and stimuli. This has powerful and tangible benefits to marketing. An Aberdeen Group study published in December 2011 found marketing organizations that applied data mining and statistical modeling to optimize marketing efforts saw as much as a 2X lift from marketing campaigns, a 76 percent higher click-through rate, and a 73 percent higher sales lift.

Marketing organizations are seeing the tremendous power and potential of predictive analytics across a broad spectrum of marketing activities. For example:

- Proactively optimizing marketing campaigns to improve engagement and conversions;
- Identifying customers most likely to switch companies and targeting offers to them designed to keep them as customers;
- Delivering customized offers designed to appeal to a prospect's specific interests or life situation; and
- Predicting which "first visit" customers are most likely to return or not return, and sending offers targeting the "not likely to return" group while avoiding the costs of making offers to those likely to return anyway.

In 2013, we have seen analytics continue to be a mainstream news subject. Analytics is only in the early migration phase from early adopters to mainstream use. Expect this trend to continue and accelerate in the coming years as more marketers discover that analytics are a clear path to improving marketing effectiveness, efficiency, and ultimately, the bottom line.

Five Social Media Measurement Questions I Hope (Not) to See in 2014

(January 2, 2014)

I get asked lots of great questions about social media measurement. Following are five not so great ones I hope not to hear in 2014.

1. *How do you measure social media?*

I get this question quite often and I enjoy it each time because if provides me the opportunity to make an important point about measurement and be a little snarky at the same time. Good stuff! When I get this question, my answer is always the same: "I don't measure 'social media,' I measure what you are trying to accomplish with social media." This may seem like I'm playing semantic games, but the distinction is very important. Measurement is fundamentally about performance against objectives. So, we measure our performance against the objectives established in the social media plan. A lot of what passes for measurement in social media is really data collection—tracking Followers or Likes, blog traffic or consumer engagement on Facebook. Unless you have measurable objectives and targets in each of these areas, you are collecting data not measuring. What do you want to happen as a result of your social media campaign or initiative? Let's measure that.

2. *How much is a Like worth?*

This question doesn't come up quite as often as in 2012, but it is still asked and, unfortunately, answered largely based on flawed logic and/or research design. You may recall the first two "research" studies attempting to answer this question, which came up with widely disparate values—somewhere around $3.14 in one case and over $100 in the other (Edwards 2013). This alone should raise major red flags. Setting the flawed research aside, trying to assign a value to a Like happens because people are desperate to assign financial value to social media and determine ROI. Those are noble things to do, but we need to focus on the other end of the customer journey—have we created engagement, has the engagement changed opinions, attitudes, beliefs, or behavior, and how those changes translate to Impact. Unless you understand the impact created by your social media program, you really can't attribute value properly. I would argue that Likes, which can be bought or gamified, really have no inherent value.

3. *Can I use a banner ad cost to calculate social media AVE?*

This question is somewhat related to the "Like worth" question in that it reflects a desire to quickly and easily assign financial value, when, in fact, assigning financial value is often hard and expensive. In this case, the questioner is attempting to take the highly flawed and discredited concept of Advertising Value Equivalency (AVE) (*more information in "AVEs [Advertising Value Equivalents] Revisited" in Chapter 5*) and apply it to social media. Where this question typically comes up is in blogger relations, where a company/brand/organization has worked with a blogger to earn "coverage" on the blog and wants to assign a financial value to the post. They would like to say that the post is worth X, with X being the cost of a banner ad on the blog (setting aside, of course, that many blogs do not accept advertising). Equating cost with value is comparing apples to oranges. First, a better practice is not to assign value to each post, but to all the posts together in a campaign. Then instead of trying to say that the campaign is worth say 14.35 ads, let's try to explain the actual impact the campaign has created on the target audience—for example, increase in awareness, increase in purchase intent, or higher propensity to purchase more often. Once you understand the impact, decide if you have the data, time, expertise, and budget to assign financial impact to the impact created.

4. *Which social media listening tool do you recommend?*

The correct answer to this question is, "it depends." This is a bad question simply because there is no one "best" social media listening tool for all circumstances and use cases. I believe you should always develop a set of platform requirements driven by the social listening stakeholders in your organization. Once these needs and requirements are understood, develop a custom request for information (RFI) designed around the specific requirements you have identified. Have each of your potential platform partners respond to the RFI; have the best respondents give you a platform demonstration according to a custom demonstration script you have developed; and pick the listening tool that best meets your unique requirements. The last three evaluations I have conducted for clients resulted in three different "winners." There is no "best social listening tool," so find the tool that meets your requirements the best.

5. *How many Impressions did we get with our latest social media campaign?*

This is not a terrible question at all unless it is the only question asked or is perceived to be the key metric for measuring social media campaign performance. Too often, organizations use Impressions as their primary social media metric instead of engagement, influence, or action-oriented metrics. Also, keep in mind that Impressions represent an opportunity to see content; they are not the actual number of people who saw the content, that number is *much* lower. Impressions always overstate the actual number of people who were exposed to your content and message.

If you plan to report on campaign impressions, please seriously consider only taking credit for those impressions that are directly against your target audience. If your target is 25 to 34-year-old males, you should only report on the impressions against this target group. Why take credit for 45 to 60-year-old female impressions when the product is not at all relevant to this audience? Target audience impressions are really what you should be concerned about and what you should be reporting. Many people know and understand this but still persist in reporting all impressions because the number is usually much larger—meaningless but larger.

If you do report on Impressions, please consider using the emerging industry standard definitions developed by The Coalition (The Conclave Social Media Measurement Standards n.d.). This will help ensure that we define Impressions consistently and don't confuse Reach with Impressions.

Social Media Metrics and Measurement Continue to Evolve

(January 9, 2014)

This week on June 11/12, AMEC is holding their next International Summit on Measurement. Many of you will recognize AMEC as the framer of the Barcelona Principles at their annual meeting in 2010. The theme this year is upping the game to deliver relevant insights along with traditional measurement reporting on performance against objectives and KPIs,[6] in

---

[6] KPIs: Key Performance Indicators.

order to provide a richer environment and context for making strategic business decisions.

In this post, I wanted to shine the light on a workshop during the Summit called *Metrics that matter: Making sense of social media measurement.* The session, led by Richard Bagnall,[7] promises to look at the latest social media measurement trends, provide a look ahead at what might be right around the corner in the next 12 months, and unveiled a revised and enhanced AMEC social media measurement framework guide that should make it easier to implement the frameworks in your own planning environments.

At last year's Summit in Madrid, we presented the initial work in developing models and frameworks to support rigorous and valid social media measurement. It consisted primarily of three elements—a new model for social media measurement, a couple of alternative ways to think about populating the model with relevant metrics, and a social media measurement planning framework/template. The initial metrics approaches focused on two alternatives, metrics focused across programmatic, channel, and business dimensions as well as an approach based on the PESO-integrated channel metrics approach, which enjoys traction in many organizations. Based on using and customizing the approach for multiple clients (see Table 1.2), here are a few things to consider as you review and think about using the new frameworks and usage guidance to be unveiled this week.

As campaigns become increasingly integrated across media types, it makes sense to also reflect this integrated view in measurement. Ideally, measurement should reflect a similar level of integration as the campaign or program being measured. As we measure performance from the four channels, we should keep in mind what we really would like to understand is how the channel efforts amplify or build on each other.

The work presented at last year's Summit showed example or illustrative metrics for each of the media types across the measurement model. Expect this year's version to take a stronger view of the most relevant or best metrics to use when employing this approach.

---

[7] Richard Bagnall is CEO of PRIME Research UK and SVP of PRIME Research Europe.

Table 1.2 PESO and exposure–engagement–influence–impact–advocacy matrix

	EXPOSURE	ENGAGEMENT	INFLUENCE	IMPACT	ADVOCACY
PAID	• Impressions • Reach • Frequency • Viewability • GRPs • TRPs • Video views • Completed views	• Engagement (paid social) • Click-throughs • Page views (page landings) • Interactions: expand, unmute, reply, enter data, etc.	• Awareness • Purchase consideration • Purchase intent • Likelihood to recommend • Brand attributes or equities	• Visit website • Attend event • Sales conversion • Download coupon • Leads captured • Promo redemption	• Mentions in Earned channel • Recommendation • Review • Ratings
OWNED	• Unique visitors • Visits	• Return visits • Page views (per visit) • Interactions: clicks, views, use tools • Subscriptions • Links	• Consideration • Purchase intent • Tell a friend • Likelihood to recommend • Brand attributes or equities	• Sales • Leads • Info requests • Download paper • Download app • Cost savings	• Recommendations • Ratings • Reviews
SHARED	• Organic impressions • Organic Reach • Number of followers	• Likes • Comments • Shares • Replies • Retweets • Etc	• Consideration • Purchase intent • Tell a friend • Likelihood to Recommend • Brand attributes or equities	• Visit store • Attend the event • Sales • Vote for issue • Satisfaction • Loyalty	• Ratings • Reviews • Recommendations • Recommendations rate
EARNED	• Number of posts • Impressions • Message delivery	• Hashtag usage • Mentions • Content entries/participants	• Awareness • Consideration • Purchase intent • Associations with issues/topics	• Visit website • Attend event • Download coupon • Leads captured • Promo redemptions	• Recommendations • Ratings • Reviews

Note: Used with permission of AMEC.

Another key development would be the presentation of different metrics models to use with the measurement model. The intention all along was that there could be a range of choices to fit different corporate cultures and planning environments.

Measurement Planning Template

The measurement planning template is the heart of your social media measurement planning effort (see Table 1.3). It is best used by conducting a facilitated discussion with all measurement stakeholders around each of the key elements in the planning template. Setting aside half a day to complete the exercise is not excessive. Here is how we think about using the template in our social media measurement planning.

Business or organizational objectives: The agreed-upon overarching organizational objective(s) the social media effort is designed to impact. These objectives may be given to the social media team or they may be the result of conversations and negotiations.

KPIs (key performance indicators): One or two high-level metrics that are aligned with the business/organizational objectives and are out-come-oriented. Again, the KPIs may be given to the measurement team or the measurement team can help guide the conversation to develop them.

Program elements: Outline the major elements of the program. The elements should reflect the scope and integration of the campaign. They could range from a simple social media program to one that includes social media, online advertising, influencer outreach, e-mail marketing, and other elements.

Table 1.3 Social media measurement planning

Business or organizational objectives	KPIs	Program elements	Program objectives	Measurement story	Key metrics

Note: Used with permission of AMEC.

Program objectives: Capture or write the measurable objective associated with each major aspect of the program. Frequently you will need to help rewrite the metrics to make them measurable. You may also need to rewrite them to actually make them objectives (what) and not strategies (how).

Measurement story: This is an attempt to marry the concepts of measurement and storytelling. At the end of the program, what measurement story would you like to be able to tell your key stakeholders? This should be based on accomplishing your specific KPIs through the success of the programs used and your ability to prove that through data and measurement. We typically develop the measurement story right after settling on the business objectives and KPIs, and use it as a guidepost to ensure that we have the means and methods to tell the desired story.

Key metrics: The metrics directly tied to program objectives. Should be aligned with the objectives as well as the higher-order KPIs. The most important KPIs and metrics are often captured on a dashboard for monitoring and reporting.

Determining the Importance of Metrics

A question sometimes comes up about the best way to determine the most important metrics—what rises to the level of inclusion on a high-level dashboard? Here are a few tips to consider:

1. *Place metrics in their respective place in the measurement model (exposure/engagement/influence/impact/advocacy).* Metrics that appear toward the right side of the model are generally more compelling than those addressing just exposure or engagement. These generally get to the outcomes rather than just outputs of program activities.
2. *Examine how closely aligned each metric is with program objectives.* Metrics that directly support the objective are generally more important than those that indirectly support the objective.
3. *Look at the degree to which the metric is explicitly part of the measurement story.* Metrics directly aligned with the measurement story represent better potential dashboard metrics than those that are tangential to the story.

4. *Metrics that provide context are generally stronger than those that don't.* For example, retweets (RTs) per 1,000 Followers tell you much more than just the number of RTs—it gives an indication of community engagement. Likewise, engagement rate (number of engagements divided by total reach) is a better metric than just the number of engagements.

5. *Remember the audience.* At the end of the day, when you're showing your stakeholders what you accomplished this year, what would they be most excited to hear? What will they want to see that ultimately demonstrates the best use of their dollars?

CHAPTER 2

Demystifying Return on Investment

Don was an amazing man, and I am very grateful that I was privileged to work with him. His legacy is a public relations industry that is infinitely better, more accountable, and more professional because of his contributions. His efforts on behalf of the IPR Measurement Commission, the Conclave on Social Media Measurement Standards, and countless other volunteer efforts that were helped by his brains and energy have changed the Public Relations field forever. Most importantly, he was able to make change and get support for his ideas with an unending supply of grace, humor, wit, and kindness. I'm grateful to have worked with him and been inspired by him. He will be forever missed but never forgotten.

—Katie Paine, CEO of Paine Publishing

This chapter includes:

- The definition of ROI (return on investment) in public relations and social media measurement
- What the ROI metrics should (and should not) be like
- The appropriate ways to measure ROI
- How to get relief from your social media ROI angst

The Difference Between Value and ROI

(June 12, 2009)

Social media and public relations programs create value and in some cases generate demonstrable ROI. The two concepts are different in important ways. They are related like the rectangle and the square. Remember that silly distinction you learned in elementary school? A square is a rectangle, but a rectangle is not a square. ROI is a form of value, but not all value takes the form of ROI.

ROI is a financial metric—percentage of dollars returned for a given investment/cost. The dollars may be revenue generated, dollars saved, or spending avoided. ROI is transactional. ROI lives on the income statement in business terms.

Value is created when people become aware of us, engage with our content or brand ambassadors, are influenced by this engagement, and take some action such as recommending to a friend or buying our product. Value creation occurs over time, not at a point in time. Value creation is process-oriented. Value lives on the balance sheet.

From a sales process perspective, the ultimate value of a social media program may be in increasing the number of people who are likely to buy our products and services. Other programs may be designed to improve or protect corporate reputation or to build and enhance brands. Much of this value is said to be *intangible*. It is goodwill that becomes tangible at the point in time a transaction occurs. When buying decisions happen, your investments in marketing, brand, and reputation work together. They become tangible. You can measure the ROI.

Many of the well-intentioned but misguided attempts to rename or reinvent what ROI means in social media—return on influence and return on engagement probably getting the most play—seem to be the result of an inability to distinguish value creation from ROI. We know that social networks have the ability to create value through customer engagement and community-building. However, ROI can only be measured by their ultimate impact on downstream metrics such as sales, employee retention, and customer loyalty/repeat purchase.

Your investments in social media or public relations remain an investment, creating additional value if done correctly, until which time they can be linked to a business outcome transaction that results in ROI.

Are you trying to get, keep, or increase your budget for social tools, people, and programs? Estimate ROI where you can, but also try to articulate the value your programs will be creating, and how this value aligns with, and contributes toward achieving one or more desired business outcomes. Propose metrics to track and assess progress in exposure, engagement, and audience influence. This is a better conversation to have than, "Let me tell you about Return on Influence ..."

Make sense?

ROI—Is Statistical Modeling the Answer?
Depends on the Question

(June 15, 2006)

Back in the saddle after much traveling and more than a few major project deadlines ... On May 23, *PRWeek* hosted a webinar with Dr. Hans Bender of Procter and Gamble, and Mark Weiner, CEO of Delahaye, discussing P&G's statistical modeling efforts to determine the ROI of public relations. First, here's a brief summary of the discussion:

- P&G employed marketing mix modeling (MMM) for six brands over a one-to-three-year period. Three of the six showed public relations with the highest ROI of any marketing tactic.
- They employed multivariate analysis that relates changes in the marketing mix (advertising, direct, public relations, etc.) to changes in business results. The basic inputs were impressions by week and sales by week.
- P&G spent $5.9B in advertising during 2005.
- Factors other than quantity/impressions were used to factor public relations impressions—primarily quality of coverage indicators such as message delivery, type of article—mention/feature/exclusive, competitor mentions, and media type (online, TV, print, radio).
- The model allows for comparison of public relations performance with other marketing tactics (advertising, direct, promotions, etc.), as well as the ability to compare various elements/campaigns within public relations.
  So what did P&G find out about public relations ROI?
- Public relations drives sales, often on a par with advertising.
- Public relations delivers stellar ROI, much greater than advertising.

- Public relations provides a halo effect over other marketing tactics.
- Overall, P&G found about a 275 percent ROI for public relations.
- Public relations delivers high ROI on relatively low levels of spending.

The last point raises an interesting question—to what degree is the ROI on public relations scalable? That is, can ROI continue at high levels with even higher levels of public relations spend? We would love to be involved with trying to answer this question with all of our clients!

In the promotion of the web event, the question was raised, "Has P&G cracked the public relations measurement code?" The short answer is "No." Not that the work they did isn't significant, interesting, and highly relevant. It's just that MMM is hardly new, particularly with consumer companies. We currently have multiple clients employing modeling that measures public relations ROI. What is new and significant about the P&G case is that they are one of the world's leading brands, and they were openly willing to share their experience and results.

MMM is an area that deserves much more attention from the public relations community. It is interesting to note the story about the P&G modeling effort broke in the advertising, not public relations, trades.

The reason why MMM is not *the* answer to proving the value of public relations is that it really only addresses the media component of public relations. One could argue about the percentage, but media relations is maybe 50 percent or a little more of what we do. Brand public relations, reputation management, public affairs, thought leadership, analyst relations, events, grass roots, and crisis communications quickly come to mind as significant areas of public relations involvement and importance where media coverage may not be the primary objective or measure of success. Modeling is also limited in that it (mostly) addresses the short-term, tangible impact of public relations. Public relations, as we know, has both short- and long-term impacts that are both tangible like sales and intangible like brand-building and reputation management. Although MMM is not *the* answer to public relations measurement, it is *one* of the answers we should be utilizing more often. For some companies with large marketing investments, diverse marketing tactics, and visibility into end sales, it may be the best answer for demonstrating ROI for public relations. Plus, since public relations almost always shows high levels of ROI and superior levels of ROI compared to most marketing tactics, it may be our best weapon to justify higher levels of public relations investment.

Marketing Mix Modeling Follow-Up

(January 12, 2007)

Last June I wrote on P&G's work with Delahaye in marketing mix modeling (MMM). There have been a lot of interesting comments, and I wanted to take a moment to answer a few questions posed by *ph hanky* in his/her January 10 comment. Here is the comment:

ph hanky—January 10, 2007

Who does P&G's MMM work anyway? Delahaye isn't a modeling agency.

The problem with companies like P&G and Delahaye making sweeping statements like this is that there is no one to audit or verify the findings. Anytime you have someone doing a regression analysis like MMM, you have to question if the regression analysis was done with the right vigor and make sure enough factors were factored in the analysis.

P&G has been making lots and lots of money and AG Laffley has been talking about their MMM and how they are cutting back on TV in favor of other vehicles. I don't doubt P&G pulls off some world-class MMM, but I don't know if they promote stuff like this to put the screws on their ad agencies and TV advertising rates.

If they spent half of what they spend on TV on public relations, then they would saturate the airwaves, the web, and print with public relations. They don't address diminishing returns on public relations. I would assume you reach saturation point with public relations long before you reach saturation on Tide commercials.

First, the easy question. The company that worked with Delahaye to develop the model is a firm called Communications Consulting Worldwide (www.ccworldwide.com).

Regarding the audit or verification of findings, my personal view is that this is not the right way to think about modeling. A properly built model should yield a highly correlated approximation of the relationship between public relations results and downstream outcomes, usually sales. There are certainly some issues that the modeling company may find uncomfortable—co-dependence of variables and reverse correlation to name two. So while there may be a little leap of faith with the model, the rigor is generally much greater than is normally applied with simple media content analysis—and the leap of faith to ROI is much shorter.

The other issue *ph hanky* raises is diminishing returns on high levels of public relations investment. In my experience we should be so lucky. I have never seen a completed model that demonstrated that public relations investments were on the diminishing returns side of the curve. On the contrary, every model that I have seen suggests that public relations investments are well below diminishing returns. If a company is spending $60 million in advertising and say $1 million in public relations (actual numbers from a former client), then the issue of diminishing returns on public relations is not applicable. Moving just $1 million from advertising to public relations would show nice leverage in ROI. I would love to be in a situation where I had to go to a client and recommend that we reduce public relations spend because we have reached diminishing returns, although I am not holding my breath on this one.

With Primary Research Secondary, Public Relations ROI Efforts Will Remain Elusive

(December 8, 2008)
A couple of months ago I was in a meeting with a client and their digital media agency. The guy from the digital agency made an offhand comment, which I thought was interesting, and hits on a key issue in public relations research and measurement. He said that he had always considered the number of posts a proxy for awareness, and the number of comments a proxy for engagement. It struck me that this notion of

measurement by proxy is actually the norm rather than the exception. Often, public relations outputs are used to assess campaign performance rather than trying to determine whether or not the campaign actually touched and moved the targets in the ways we intended. The continued industry reliance on the use of advertising value equivalents (AVEs) is perhaps the most common misuse of the measurement by proxy notion. AVEs are an attempt to determine ROI by proxy.

We need more measurement by fact, not by proxy. We need to move beyond just measuring what the public relations result is (a hit, an OTS,[1] a delivered message) to measuring what the public relations result actually accomplished—did we reach the intended targets; did they engage with the content; did we cause them to rethink existing perceptions; did we change their attitudes; did we increase the likelihood that they would consider the brand? In order to move toward measurement by fact, a much greater emphasis on primary audience research is necessary. As an industry, we would be well-served by a higher commitment to primary research. Research allows us to shift the conversation from measurement by implication (i.e., x percent of the coverage contained a key message and therefore the campaign was a success) to measurement by fact (e.g., 10 percent of the target audience saw the public relations campaign and 15 percent of these individuals plan to purchase the product in the next six months). Rather than using content links or the comments to posts ratio as a proxy for brand engagement, wouldn't it be better to do primary research designed to measure how engaged and attached online consumers actually are to the brand and why? Importantly, efforts to determine the ROI of public relations are greatly enabled by primary research. The better we actually understand whether or not public relations has influenced the consumer and what actions, if any, they take as a result, the better we can assess the true ROI of a campaign.

There are three inhibitors to the expanded use of primary research in public relations measurement—education, lack of vendor focus, and perceived high costs. Many public relations professionals lack the education and training to feel confident that they know where and when to use

---

[1] Editor: OTS: Opportunities to See (Stacks and Bowen 2013, 21).

primary research in their measurement efforts. From a research vendor perspective, there are research silos of media content analysis firms and primary research firms. While many firms offer both, their focus usually is in one area or the other. And very few firms are actively attempting to use quantitative research together with content analysis to more holistically measure public relations. Yes, primary research is generally more expensive than content analysis. However, I have seen content analysis systems costs in excess of $500K per year—you can do a lot of primary research for a fraction of that. In 2009 if the public relations industry spends about the same amount on primary research as we do in media measurement, we'll be making great progress toward measurement by fact.

ROI Is to Public Relations as PER Is to the NBA[2]?

(April 19, 2006)

This is a guest post from my research and measurement colleague at GCI, Wilson Tan.

Public relations is not the only industry in search of the holy grail of ROI. This past Saturday's *Weekend Journal* profiled the NBA's search for their breakthrough statistic (Adams 2006). Statistics happy MLB has fallen in love with VORP (value over replacement player). It measures how much a hitter or pitcher contributes compared with a fictitious replacement player with average skills. Here are two metrics in play with the NBA:

Plus–minus rating: How many more or fewer points than the opponent a team scores when that player is in the game

Player efficiency rating (PER): Measures a player's per-minute productivity using both positive contributions (such as assists) and negative ones (such as missed shots)

The NBA also has some of the same challenges as public relations in understanding intangible value. Sonics's CEO Wally Walker says the team's fortunes this year (poor compared to last year) show that statistics

---

[2] Editor: PER—player efficiency rating; NBA—The National Basketball Association.

are hardly a panacea. "Our chemistry isn't nearly as good this year as it was last year," he says. "It's hard to hang a number on that."

If the NBA, in an enclosed arena of 94 by 50 feet, has a struggle defining a breakthrough statistic, no wonder that we in public relations struggle with the much bigger arena of the real world.

Oh, Canada—Is MRP the Answer?

(April 27, 2006)

On April 20, the Canadian Public Relations Society (CPRS) unveiled the media relations rating points (MRP) system, an attempt to come up with a single metric for media relations measurement. Here are a few initial impressions.

Use of Public Relations Multiplier Hurts Credibility

The MRP uses a multiplier of 2.5 on circulation figures to arrive at impressions. Advocates for the use of multipliers argue that one of two positions—either public relations impressions are "worth more" than other (i.e., advertising) impressions due to editorial credibility, or they are accounting for pass-along readership in addition to base circulation. Neither position is defensible or advisable. The only credible, consistent way to report impressions is by using audited circulation or audience figures. I know of no industry association or governing body (e.g., PRSA) that supports the use of a multiplier. It is bad business for the public relations industry.

MRP Is NOT ROI

I guess the CPRS Measurement Committee could not resist using the magic measurement acronym—ROI—to describe the MRP. This is spin. The MRP uses a cost per impression metric, which is preferable to just impressions and does allow comparison to advertising, but it does not give ROI. ROI has become one of the most misused terms in public relations. In order to calculate a true ROI, you compare the dollar value of what is created (sales, perception changes, etc.) to the cost of doing it. Cost per impression is just that, a cost-oriented metric, not value-oriented. It does not give ROI.

Are All MRPs the Same?

The fact that one selects five qualitative factors from a longer list to include in the MRP for a given campaign seems to mean that for five different campaigns all reporting MRPs, you could have five slightly different ways of scoring articles for the index. I am not sure how meaningful this is, but it does seem to raise possible issues around consistency of application of the metric. I also found it a little odd that no attempt was made to weigh the various factors according to their ability to impact the readers as determined by primary research.

Where's the Public Relations Proof?

For any single metric to be compelling, you would like to know how it correlates to desired business outcomes. Does the metric show statistical correlation to some desired "downstream" behavior—sales, likelihood to buy or recommend the stock, brand preference or prescription volume, for example? It is hard to tell if any of this sort of research has been undertaken by the MRP sponsors. I did not find any evidence of it.

It's always easier to criticize than create, so I applaud the efforts of the CPRS and the MRP Committee. This was a massive undertaking and they accomplished a lot to get to this point. The MRP is not a magic bullet, and may be fatally flawed. But who knows—it may take off in Canada and prove to be a valuable tool. Should be fun to watch!

Update on MRPs

(April 27, 2006)

I wanted to acknowledge a factual error in my April 24 post (*Oh Canada—Is MRP the Answer?*) regarding the use of a multiplier in the new MRP system championed by the CPRS. The system does not currently use a multiplier as Rachel Douglas, a member of the CPRS Measurement Committee, points out in her comment to the post. Thank you Rachel. Good news and a good decision by the committee.

In my defense, the presentation from the CPRS on the MRP I saw, dated March 2, 2006, clearly called for the use of the multiplier. I'm glad that this was changed prior to the official launch on April 20.

I stand by the rest of my comments including the misuse of "ROI" in describing the MRP metric.

In Social Media, Are We Looking for ROI in All the Wrong Places?

(May 28, 2009)

One of the hotter topics in my corner of the Twitterverse is ROI. How do you calculate the ROI of social media? What's the ROI of Twitter? The questions are many, the answers are too few. There have been several blog posts on the subject, and I plan to post an overview and synthesis of some of the better ones in the near future. One important question seems to be missing from much of the conversation: To what degree should social media be considered a cost of doing business (from a corporate/organizational viewpoint) rather than a distinct activity that must/should be justified by hard ROI?

If your customers want the option of customer service via Twitter do you really have an option long term? If crises are often spawned in social media, how optional is listening/monitoring if you want to protect your brand? Increasingly, the corporate world will realize that the options are all with the consumers/customers and how, how often, what, and why we communicate will largely be in response to this dynamic. When voicemail came on the scene (patented in 1983), I'm sure the ROI pencils were sharpened and presentations were made. When was the last time someone was asked to justify the cost of voice messaging or 800 numbers or e-mail? They are all considered part of the cost of doing business today. In a relatively short period I believe that many applications of social media—CRM,[3] crisis monitoring, listening to customers/competitors/industry voices, and many others—will be considered necessary, baseline activities to doing business in the 21st century.

---

[3] Editor: CRM: Customer Relationship Management.

The ability and need to demonstrate ROI in social media should be considered contextual and dependent on specific program/initiative objectives. If the objective is "listening and learning," what's the ROI on insight? However, in other cases, program objectives will be to drive a specific business outcome, and demonstrating ROI will be expected and required if budgets are to follow. Dell offering product promotions on Twitter was closed-loop and easy to calculate ROI. HyperLocal marketing by Kogi or your local pizza shop on Twitter is measureable in incremental sales. You can calculate the ROI on a hotel or resort offering last-minute cut-rate weekends via Facebook.

Knowing when social media should be considered part of the cost of doing business and making this case to your company or clients may just make the ROI imperative a little less urgent and more focused in the right areas.

Five Things You Should Know About Social Media ROI

(June 8, 2009)

In a January post of 2009 social media predictions (*more information in article "Five public relations and social media measurement trends to watch in 2009" in Chapter 1*) I wrote:

In 2009, the pendulum will swing from experimentation to accountability. This year will raise the bar on all of us to demonstrate how social media and public relations programs are helping to drive desired business outcomes.

Are you seeing the accountability bar being raised this year? In my corner of the world, the volume of conversation about social media ROI is high and accelerating. Unfortunately, much of the conversation has been misinformed and misguided. It seems like every week brings another post attempting to reinvent the acronym or the meaning—ROI really means Return on Influence, or Return on Engagement is the new ROI, and on and on. There is another group of online Zen Masters who would have you believe that social media ROI is old school thinking and not in tune with social media Zeitgeist. In that case, I'll take "Old School" for $100, please.

Here are five things about social media ROI you should know:

1. *ROI is a financial metric.* It tells the percentage of financial return you generated for a given investment level. The financial return is usually revenue, but may also be money you saved by making the investment or money you avoided spending in the future. Notice the common thread here—it's about money.

2. *Attempts to reinvent the acronym are counterproductive.* Return on Influence/Engagement/whatever; do not ever get to the basic money question. Most of these attempts share two characteristics—they are confusing "return" with impact/results, and/or they are making an argument that social media ROI is largely intangible, presented by relationships, engagement, and community. What they are really saying, perhaps unintentionally, is that ROI is often difficult to determine and I really don't understand it. In my opinion, attempts to reinvent or circumvent ROI discussion in social media actually hurt credibility with the people writing the checks. They expect an apples-to-apples—money in and money out—discussion.

3. *ROI in social media has a time dimension.* Value may be created in the short term and longer term. Social media-specific promotions are an example of easily measured and short-term ROI. Longer-term value is much more difficult to quantify. There are some similarities between social media and brand in this regard. Success in each is a process and not an event. You generally will have ongoing activities that sustain the brand/social media program and brand-building events or campaigns that provide short-term spikes in awareness and engagement. Contribution to organic search results is another example of longer-term value creation with branding and social media efforts. Managing and measuring your social media effort properly requires thinking about the value you are creating in the short and longer term.

4. *Linkage and correlations are important.* In order to demonstrate ROI in social media, it is necessary to link the results seen in social media with the relevant business processes they are addressing. For

example, in a B2B company, you might try to link social media efforts with the lead generation and closure process. For a program aimed at employee engagement, you might link social media efforts to the employee recruitment and retention business process. For an e-commerce company you might be able to directly link to the sales process through unique URLs or click-tracking technologies. When attempting to show statistical relationships, correlations become important. We might try to correlate social media brand engagement and audience influence with metrics such as likelihood to recommend to a friend, likelihood to seriously consider the product, or likelihood to purchase the product in the next X months.

5. *All ROI studies are custom-made.* The simple fact is that you cannot buy an off-the-shelf solution to calculate the ROI of your social media effort. All ROI studies are custom-made. This is primarily a reflection of the unique objectives each company may have for their social media efforts. Objectives are specific and contextual, and your ROI measurement efforts will need to be as well. Attempts to develop ROI calculators, where you simply plug in several numbers and hit a button to calculate your ROI, are not worth the time it takes to plug in the data. They are a one-size-fits-none approach to ROI.

We are in the very early stages in our ability to measure the ROI of social media. Not enough cycles yet. Case studies are limited but growing. The need to demonstrate a financial return on social media investment, if not here already, will be here shortly. We have a lot of work to do. Let's get started.

Social Media ROI Part 1: Framework

(October 6, 2009)

Here is a simple, five-step framework for developing a social media ROI measurement program. Remember that not all social media initiatives will result in short-term ROI generation. It is also important to comprehend the results of programs that result in nonfinancial value or impact *(for a quick refresher on the difference between value and ROI, read article "The Differences between Value and ROI" in Chapter 2)*. Holistic measurement programs should be designed to track and measure nonfinancial impact as well as ROI.

1. *Set measurable objectives aligned with business outcomes*

   Failure to begin with measurable objectives is probably the most common impediment to proper social media measurement. A couple of award seasons ago I was a judge for a major public relations campaign competition and was appalled by the low percentage of programs that actually contained measurable objectives—about 20 percent or so. Your objectives should be aligned with one or more desired business outcomes. Think through all the ways in which the social business effort will contribute toward driving the overall business forward. Make sure that the alignment is obvious and understood by all involved in program approval.

2. *Link to and understand the requisite business process*

   In order to demonstrate ROI in social media it is necessary to link the results seen in social media with the relevant business processes they are addressing. Social programs to date generally relate to one or more of the following business processes (Table 2.1):

Table 2.1 Public relations business processes

Business process	Description
CRM	Crowd-sourced help, info, recommendations, customer relationships
Research	Competitive intelligence, insights, voice-of-customer, trends, feedback, reputation assessment, influencers
Marketing and sales	Ideation, product promotion, hyper-local marketing, lead generation and closure, fund raising, testing, brand attributes
Communication/Public relations/Investor relations	Stakeholder communication (internal and external)
Innovation/Product development	Crowd-sourced ideas, problem/opportunity identification, collaboration

For example, in a B2B company, you might try to link social media efforts with the lead generation and closure process as represented in Figure 2.1.

For a program aimed at employee engagement, you might link social media efforts to the employee recruitment and retention business process. For an e-commerce company you might be able to directly link to the sales process through unique URLs or click-tracking technologies as represented in Figure 2.2.

Understanding which business processes are impacted by social networks, and how, is fundamental to understanding ROI.

3. *Select communications model, research approach, and key metrics*

In addition to understanding the business process impacted by social programs, it is important to have a communications model to assess nonfinancial impact. The accepted Outputs→Outtakes→Outcomes communication model is difficult and confusing for many to understand and apply. Here is an alternative communication model that is somewhat more intuitive and in tune with social media measurement (see Figure 2.3).

- *Exposure*—To what degree have we created exposure to content and message?
- *Engagement*—Who is interacting/engaging with our content? How and where?
- *Influence*—The degree to which exposure and engagement have influenced perceptions and attitudes of the target audience.

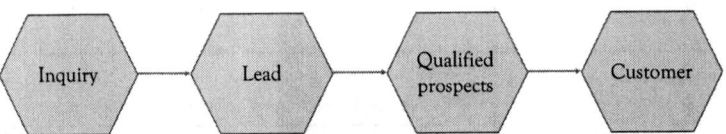

Figure 2.1 Social media efforts to customer

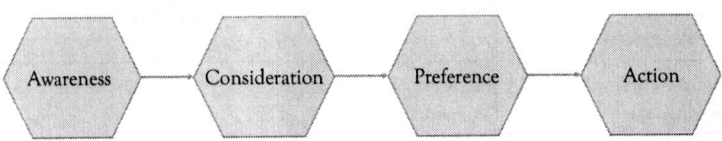

Figure 2.2 Employee awareness to action

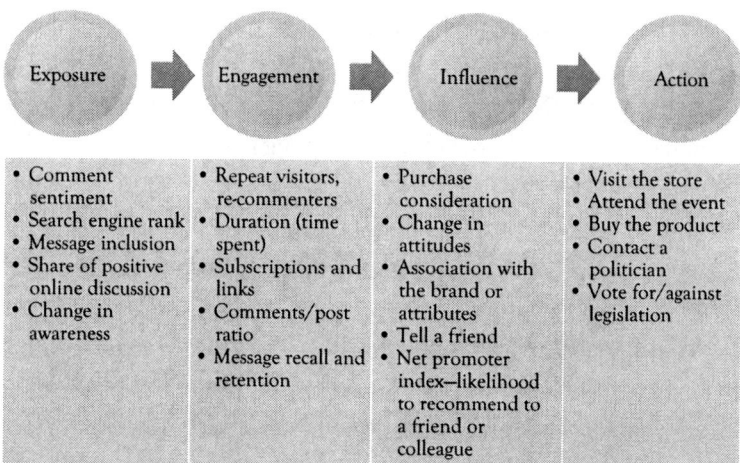

Figure 2.3 Exposure–engagement–influence–action model

- *Action*—As a result of the social media effort, what actions if any has the target taken?

The metrics listed are a starting point. You will note that these metrics come from all three "zones of measurement"—(*more information in article "A 30000-Foot View of Social Media Measurement" in Chapter 4*)—web analytics, digital content analysis, and primary audience research. Possible ROI research approaches include:

- Correlation modeling and econometrics
- Staff cost reduction and/or cost elimination tracking
- Direct linkage via unique URLs and click-tracking
- Exposed/Not-exposed primary audience research
- Integrated cross-platform research—web analytics, content analysis, click tracking, primary research

4. *Gather and analyze data*

Gather longitudinal data for the requisite business process and communication model metrics. When attempting to show statistical correlations, the amount of data you include is important because it impacts the confidence level of the results. Also, what metrics you attempt to correlate and how is crucial. For example, we might try to correlate social media brand engagement and audience influence with metrics such as likelihood to recommend to a friend, likelihood to seriously consider the product, or likelihood to purchase the product in the next X months. Select the metrics that are most applicable to the business process you are attempting to drive.

5. *Calculate ROI and report results*

We started with measurable objectives, aligned them with requisite business processes, determined our research model and approach, and have gathered the data. Now we can calculate ROI and describe the value of the social business initiative. Results for key program metrics should be captured on a dashboard that may be shared with all program stakeholders on a regular basis.

Social Media ROI Part 2: Research Approaches

(October 8, 2009)

In Part 1, we attempted to define a framework for thinking about measuring the ROI of social media activities and programs. In this post we'll take a relatively high-level view of specific research approaches that are applicable to calculating social business ROI.

One of the items that I stress to my public relations/advertising research students is the need for a researcher to understand the industry/business in which they are operating, how the discipline (e.g., public relations or advertising) works as well as how the specific program or initiative is designed to "work." Two baseline concepts of the ROI Framework presented in Part 1 are the need to establish measurable objectives, and that these objectives should tie to one or more relevant business processes. Alignment is crucial here and must be addressed as part of the planning process, not post-execution.

At the risk of throwing out a less than fully fleshed-out idea (OK, I am, so let's improve it together), here is a table to help you think through possible ways to align social programs. Table 2.2 shows the business functions/departments, a few possible uses of social programs in each area, the applicable business process, a few sample metrics, and the basis (revenue, cost savings, cost avoidance) for creating ROI.

Table 2.2 Metrics for creating ROI

Business Function	Uses of social media	Business process or model	Metrics	ROI basis
Customer service and support	Input, crowd-sourced help, info, recommendations, customer relationships	Customer relationship management (CRM), customer retention/loyalty, break/fix	Response time, resolution percentage, loyalty	Support and service cost savings
Research/listening	Competitive intelligence, insights, voice of customer (VOC), industry trends, feedback, influencers, crisis monitoring, first responders, reputation assessment	Competitive analysis, crisis response	Actionable ideas, association with key attributes	Reduced research costs, cost reduction
Marketing	E-commerce, ideation, product promotion, hyper-local, lead generation, fund raising, experimental/testing, brand communication	Sales funnel (awareness, consideration, preference, action, loyalty), lead generation, brand pyramid (awareness, relevance, preference, loyalty, affinity)	Awareness, purchase consideration, brand preference, number of leads, lead closure rate, brand affinity	Revenue generation
Communication/public relations	Internal/external stakeholder communication	Communication model (exposure, engagement, influence, action)	Reach, perceptions and attitudes, net promoters	Revenue generation
Innovation/product development	Crowd-sourcing, problem/opportunity identification, collaboration, ideation	Product development	Actionable ideas, time-to-market	Cost reduction

ROI Research Approaches

Direct linkage—This approach is most applicable to social media promotional or e-commerce efforts. It generally involves use of unique URLs tied to specific social networks that direct respondents to a company e-commerce website to redeem coupons or purchase product. Using this approach, Dell generated over 2 million dollars in incremental sales on their outlet site primarily driven by offers to their over 625 thousand Twitter followers. Direct linkage approaches mitigate two potential problems with ROI determination—tying the offer directly to an action and isolating the impact of each marketing channel. Web analytics should provide the data necessary to determine ROI.

Staff cost reduction—The CRM or customer service and support functions are one of the more interesting uses of social networks. There is some early work (e.g., Forrester Research n.d.) showing how social programs may directly reduce staff necessary for customer service and support; for example, when questions can be answered by other customers and not just by the company. ROI determination involves demonstrating how social programs have reduced staffing costs and call center investment requirements. ROI may also be generated by enhanced customer loyalty resulting in higher average transaction volumes or more frequent purchases.

Correlation[4] modeling and econometrics—Correlation models use statistical techniques to show the relationship between two variables of interest. For example, we may be interested in how changes in Net Promoter Score correlate with sales. The primary challenge with a correlation model is isolating the impact of social media from all the other ways—word-of-mouth (WOM), advertising, promotions, and public relations—the change in the variable of interest may have occurred. The simplest approach is to collect data during times of low or no other communication activity.

---

[4] Editor: Correlation is "a statistical test that examines the relationships between variables (may be either categorical or continuous); measures the degrees to which variables are interrelated" (Stacks and Bowen 2015, 7). Different from regression which is "a statistical tool that predicts outcomes based on one outcome (dependent) variable and one predictor (independent) variable" (Stacks and Bowen 2013, 26), correlation analysis does not assume causality reasoning.

If multiple communication channels are in use, econometric models that attempt to statistically isolate the impact of each communication variable should be used. Econometric modeling is expensive (in the ballpark of $100K to develop a model) and is data sensitive. That is, a lot of data is generally required for the models to work properly. One also needs a lot of data (generally model designers want two or three years' worth of data to isolate effects such as seasonality) in order to achieve sufficiently high confidence levels in the correlation. Other challenges include data normalization and the estimation of the baseline level of sales, which is defined as the sales that would occur in the absence of any promotion or marketing. For retail econometric models with established brands, the baseline sales might be around 50 percent of the observed volume.

I prefer models that attempt to correlate public relations/social media outputs to public relations/social media outcomes, and then a second correlation involving public relations/social media outcomes (e.g., purchase consideration or Net Promoter) with business outcomes such as sales. Here is a simplified overview of a possible modeling approach (see Figure 2.4).

Econometric models have two important characteristics—They are predictive, so once you develop a model, in the absence of changes in the assumptions, they may be used for forecasting without the need to generate new models, and it provides a way to address value attribution for nonfinancial indicators such as exposure, engagement, or influence.

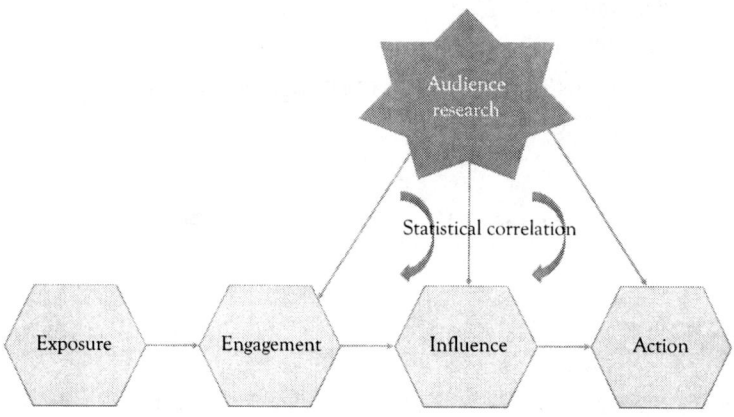

Figure 2.4 Possible public relations model

Exposed/Not exposed—This form of research attempts to identify those individuals within your target audience who were exposed to programs and content, and compare their purchase intent or purchase history with a control group of audience members who were not exposed to the program and content. The "lift" created within the exposed group is used to calculate ROI. The research approach involves use of primary audience research to gather the data necessary to calculate ROI. You would screen respondents for exposure to specific social programs (this is tricky from a research questionnaire perspective) using visual cues and/or descriptions, being as specific as possible. Experience shows that the percentage of the potential audience exposed to a given program may be fairly low. Therefore, you may need a large sample size to net enough "exposed" respondents to have a statistically projectable sample. This dynamic drives higher research costs of course.

Integrated, cross-platform research—By utilizing a combination of web analytics, click-tracking, digital content analysis, sales/scan data, and primary research, it is possible to track behavior of individuals across websites and social networks. Companies such as Compete and ComScore are becoming more integrated in their offerings along these lines, combining online behavioral tracking with panel research. Early efforts have focused on using a combination of click-tracking, primary research, and sales scan data to track opinion, behavior, actions, and transactions. The effort undertaken by ComScore and Dunnhumby to measure MySpace advertising (Neff 2009) is a great early example of the cross-platform approach to ROI determination.

We are still in the early stages of understanding ROI with social business programs. I look forward to continuing the journey with you. Thanks for reading!

Relief from Social Media ROI Angst

(February 25, 2010)

ROI is one of the most discussed and agonized-over topics in social business today. However, much of the discussion around social media ROI has been simply confused, confusing, or misguided. There have been posts on large, well-known blogs (riff on ways to prepare potatoes) that are incredibly naive in their discussion of ROI. In some circles there is endless philosophic debate bounded on one side by the Puritans who believe that ROI is an old/incorrect way to think social business and on the other side by the Analyticans who seem to believe that you can always determine ROI with a web analytics package.

The net–net of all this is a lot of frustration, even angst over how to think about ROI, and social business. We're here to help. Take two deep breaths and read these four points. You'll feel better soon.

Point Number One: As a practical matter, the majority of social business efforts will not result in true ROI (in the short term).

In fact, I would guess far less than half will, maybe less than 10 percent. But that doesn't mean that the social business effort was not successful, or did not create significant value for the brand or organization. It simply means that the primary objectives of most social business efforts are centered on concepts such as community-building, engagement, listening, and participating in conversations. It is difficult and expensive to attribute financial value to these areas. To use the old saying—the ROI on these sorts of ROI efforts is not good. Traditional public relations, branding, and reputation programs suffer from some of the same challenges. So when a study such as the one published by e-Marketer suggests "only" 16 percent of social business programs are measuring ROI (e-Marketer 2009), while many are surprised that it isn't higher, it actually sounds a little too high to me. I wonder how respondents were thinking about and defining ROI.

Point Number Two: Loose use of the term ROI is a major cause of angst.

ROI is not synonymous with results, key performance indicators (KPIs), or value. ROI is not the only or perhaps even the most relevant way to define success in social business. ROI is a financial metric. ROI can only be measured in terms of revenue generated, cost savings, or costs avoided. It is *transactional* in nature. There is ample evidence on twitter, blog posts, and in blog comments that many people say ROI when they really mean results or value.

Many of the well-intentioned but misguided attempts to rename or reinvent what ROI means in social media—return on influence and return on engagement probably getting the most play—seem to be the result of an inability to distinguish value creation from ROI.

Point Number Three: Understand the difference between value and ROI.

Social media efforts may create financial impact (ROI) and/or nonfinancial impact. Engagement and Influence are examples of nonfinancial impact. Other nonfinancial impacts such as increased brand awareness or purchase consideration may eventually result in ROI at a point in the future when a financial event occurs. Try to be explicit as to whether the social business program is designed to generate nonfinancial impact or true financial ROI, and make sure that the people writing the checks understand the difference. Show how the effort is linked to one or more business processes and how it will deliver value by helping to drive the desired business outcomes.

We know that social networks have the ability to create value through customer engagement and community-building. However, ROI can only be measured by their ultimate impact on downstream metrics such as sales, employee retention, and customer loyalty/repeat purchase. Many social business efforts are in an investment phase. The value is largely intangible. Some may eventually become transactional and result in true financial ROI.

Point Number Four: ROI in social business has a time dimension.

Value may be created in the short term and longer term. Social business campaigns utilizing channel-specific URLs and e-commerce landing pages are an example of easily measured short-term ROI (setting aside last-click attribution issues). Longer-term value is much more difficult to quantify. There are some similarities between social media and brand in this regard. Success in each is a process and not an event. You may have ongoing activities that sustain the brand/social business program and brand-building events or campaigns that provide short-term spikes in awareness and engagement. Managing and measuring your social business effort properly requires thinking about the value you are creating in the short and longer term.

Your investments in social media or public relations remain an investment, creating additional value if done correctly, until which time they can be linked to a business process transaction that results in ROI. Calculate ROI whenever you can, but also try to articulate the value your programs will be creating, and how this value aligns with, and contributes toward, achieving one or more desired business outcomes.

How Much Does a House Cost?

(November 8, 2010)

I don't come from the "there are no dumb questions" school. For example, in an academic environment, I would define a "dumb question" as one in which the answer should be easily known, had the student read the assignment or attended the previous class. There are a lot of dumb questions asked all the time and social media gets more than its share of these. Many of them are specific to social media measurement/ROI. For example:

- Which has higher ROI, Twitter or Facebook?
- What ROI should I expect from Twitter?
- How do I measure the ROI of social media?

The flip answer to all these questions is, *it depends*. All results are contextual. Results are also specific. While industry averages may be interesting, averages mask any real meaning for an individual brand or company. They result in "one size fits none" thinking. Let's go back to our house analogy and bring this to life. The cost of a house depends on several factors:

- Where is the house located? You'll need to know the city and the specific neighborhood. You may also want to know which block the house is on within a given neighborhood.
- How large is the house in terms of square feet?
- How large is the lot?
- Is the house new or previously owned?
- In what condition is the house?

- What is the level of finish-out? For example, granite versus tile countertops. High-end appliances or mid-range?
- What are the desirable or unique features of the house?

In social media measurement we have our own list of questions to ask before attempting to answer generally stated questions about measurement and ROI:

- What brand/company are we speaking about? The answers for a well-established cult brand will be very different from those of a less well-established brand. Answers for e-commerce companies will vary from those of B2B companies. Answers will also vary by industry segment.
- How long has the brand/company been participating in social networks?
- How much investment in social media marketing—time and money—has the brand/company made? What has been the level of effort?
- What other communication channels (e.g., advertising, direct, search, public relations) are being utilized in parallel with social marketing?
- What is our point of view on the role of social media in the marketing mix? For example, is the role of social media primarily to drive exposure to content or is the program or initiative designed to drive conversion events through social channels?
- What were/are the specific objectives of the program or initiative?

This last question is especially important because measurement is fundamentally about assessing performance against stated objectives. When someone asks you how to measure something in social media, your first response should always be this question—what were the specific objectives of the program or initiative?

The question of when to expect a return on social media efforts is also an interesting one. Brands often expect an immediate ROI on social media efforts. Social media marketing is a process, not an event. Too often people forget about the "I" aspect of ROI—you usually have to make an *investment* in resources and time before you can drive a return. It is wise to listen to social conversations before engaging, and build your presence and trust before trying to drive conversion events. Listen and learn and then convert. I would argue that the majority of social media efforts today are likely in the investment phase and not the return phase. It is somewhat unfair in these cases for the social media effort to be held to an ROI standard in the short term. Measuring impact rather than ROI is advised. Perhaps we can add another question to our list of dumb social media ROI questions—"What ROI should we expect in the first year of our social media initiative?"

If you are one of the prescient humans who has a crystal ball that enables you to answer the "how much does a house cost" question, I have another question for you, "how long is a string?"

CHAPTER 3

"Puzzles" Versus "Pieces"— Getting the Metrics Right

Don was as an outstanding professional who gave a lot to his firm, and he gave freely of his gifts and his time to AMEC. Without Don, who joined up with Richard Bagnall, we would not have the AMEC social media measurement framework, which is a breakthrough for our industry.

—Barry Leggetter, CEO of the International Association for the Measurement and Evaluation of Communication (AMEC)

This chapter includes:

- The differences between the "puzzles" and "pieces" in measurement
- What metrics are solving the "puzzles" versus what are merely calculating the "pieces"
- The definition and measurement of influence in social media
- The AMEC Social Media Valid Framework and how it can be applied in social media measurement

Measure the Puzzle Not the Pieces

(May 1, 2010)

A while back, I remember someone posting a question to a LinkedIn discussion group along the lines of, "I just got my client a hit in *USA Today*. How much is that worth?" More recently, *AdWeek* ran an article titled "Value of a Fan on Facebook: $3.60," citing an attempt by Vitrue to essentially assign a media value to a Facebook Fan. (Sidebar: Is a Liker worth as much as a Fan?) Setting aside an argument of the value attribution methodology used by Vitrue (I'm not a fan, or a liker), the fundamental issue I have with each example is the same; they are trying to measure the pieces and not the puzzle.

A media hit, a tweet, gaining a Fan/Liker, or obtaining a Follower are all pieces to a larger puzzle called a social media/business campaign, initiative, effort, or program. For simplicity, let's refer to them as programs henceforth. Programs have, or should have, objectives. Done correctly, these objectives are measurable. Good measurement practice suggests that you assess performance against stated objectives. Sure, it is also important to assess performance of program strategies and tactics—primarily as a diagnostic—but ultimately we must measure performance against objectives. This is a base condition for accountability.

Gaining media coverage, sending tweets or getting others to tweet about you, creating Likers or gaining Followers should be thought of as strategies, or perhaps tactics. Objectives are what you want to happen as a result of the combination of strategies and tactics. Programs are not made of single media hits, tweets, Likers, or Followers. They are longitudinal, holistic, and integrated. Successful programs might generate hundreds of media hits, scores of blog posts, and thousands of Likers or Followers. Orchestrated correctly, all these strategies and tactics should help us achieve our overall program objectives. The reality of the situation is any one discrete result of a campaign—a hit, Liker, or Follower for example—usually has a very small overall impact. The impact most likely would not be measurable, and if it was, it would not likely be meaningful. They are just pieces of the overall program puzzle.

Let's conclude with a simplistic Facebook program example. Your tactic is to gain more Likers who meet a certain demographic profile. Your strategies are to create an engaged brand community in Facebook, and to encourage online and offline word-of-mouth (WOM) about the brand. Your objective is to increase brand preference from 17 to 21 percent in the next 12 months. Measure this objective, and if you want to do value attribution and calculate return on investment (ROI), figure out how much each 1 percent increase in brand preference is worth in incremental sales. That's a puzzle worth solving.

Let's Put Outputs, Outtakes, and Outcomes in the Outhouse

(November 1, 2007)

In October, I attended the fifth Annual Summit on Measurement sponsored by the Institute for Public Relations. One of the speakers showed a chart listing public relations Outputs and Outcomes. He listed press releases as an Output rather than Impressions, Number of Hits, Message Pick-up, or any of the other metrics correctly referred to as Outputs (see the *Dictionary of Public Relations Measurement and Research*) (Stacks and Bowen 2013). Why bring this minor transgression up? Because this is not an isolated occurrence. Many public relations professionals, even senior people, regularly have to pause for a moment to make sure they don't get their Outputs confused with their Outtakes or Outcomes. Outtakes is not often used in the United States. It seems much more prevalent in Europe. The terminology is confusing and is defined in different ways by different professionals. Further compounding the confusion is the fact that the audiences we present our results or requests to rarely understand the terms and have trouble relating to them. In short, the terms are too much "inside baseball."

What we need is a metrics taxonomy that is easier to understand and explain, perhaps simple and descriptive enough that we could skip the need for explanation altogether. I propose the following three terms:

- *Exposure*—to what degree have we created exposure to materials and message?
- *Influence*—the degree to which exposure has influenced perceptions and attitudes.
- *Action*—as a result of the public relations effort, what actions if any has the target taken?

The E–I–A (Exposure–Influence–Action) construct is easy to understand and does a reasonable job of describing what we are trying to accomplish in public relations. Figure 3.1 is a graphic illustration that brings it to life a bit.

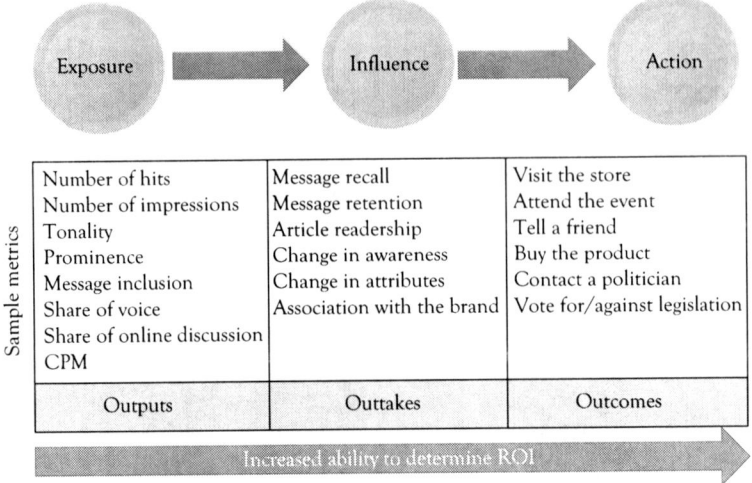

Outputs	Outtakes	Outcomes
Number of hits Number of impressions Tonality Prominence Message inclusion Share of voice Share of online discussion CPM	Message recall Message retention Article readership Change in awareness Change in attributes Association with the brand	Visit the store Attend the event Tell a friend Buy the product Contact a politician Vote for/against legislation

Figure 3.1 EIA graphic

There are lots of possible answers to this problem. EIA may be one of them. It would be great to hear whether or not you share the view that Outputs/Outtakes/Outcomes is problematic and what solutions you might offer in response.

Reach Makes a Better Impression

(March 31, 2008)

Question: You are about to go into a meeting with the C-suite members of your company to report on the success of your public relations campaign. Would you rather be able to say:

A. The campaign is working well, we have generated over 12 million impressions

or

B. The campaign is working well, we have reached 91 percent of our target audience an average of 4.2 times.

OK, so it would have been best to be able to report a direct causal link between public relations activities and sales with an estimated ROI of 250 percent, but, between the two examples, most of us would rather have reach and frequency data than just impressions. Reach is typically expressed as a percentage of the audience and therefore requires the professional to know the total audience size and how many of the audience were "reached" with a given combination of articles. You also need to understand media consumption dynamics. In the advertising world this sort of analysis is common and expected.

The power of reach is that it provides a much more realistic estimate of possible impact than impressions. For example, if you are targeting women and get a hit in the *New York Times*, most public relations pros today would lay claim to nearly 5 million impressions. Some, citing pass-along readership and/or a mythical public relations credibility advantage, might even inflate this number by a factor of three and claim almost 15 million impressions. In fact, you have reached a little less than 2 million women with the *New York Times* hit. Reach paints a more realistic picture.

In the United Kingdom, Metrica purports to have reach and frequency data gleaned from a primary study of 12,000 consumers. They use it as a standard metric in their bespoke media content analysis offering. So why don't any of the U.S.-based media content analysis firms offer reach and frequency metrics? The database development would be expensive but uptake most likely would be strong.

While both impressions and reach only represent opportunities to see (OTS), at least the reach approach requires the potential reader to be someone who could actually buy your product or service. Baby steps of progress. Next, perhaps we'll start to measure people who actually saw an article and took the time to read it. Maybe we'll use the word du jour and call these "authentic impressions."

Inflationary Twitter Audience Numbers Hurt Social Media Credibility

(July 6, 2009)

In yesterday's *New York Times*, you may have read the article "Spinning the Web: P.R. in Silicon Valley," an interesting although not overly insightful piece (Miller 2009). From a social media measurement perspective, two items caught my eye. The first, referring to Brian Solis, Principal of *FutureWorks*, about how he calculates social media audience figures:

> Instead of calculating the impressions an article gets by estimating a publication's circulation and pass-along rate, Mr. Solis counts the number of people who tweeted about a company and their combined following, the number of retweets or clicks on links, as well as traffic from Facebook and other social networks.

Toward the end of the article, we learn: "By 6:30 p.m. on the day Wordnik went live, Brew's staff calculated that 1.43 million people had seen tweets about it."

Setting aside for a moment that the article and these sorts of audience metrics take a broadcast-oriented view of Twitter (Mr. Solis discusses the shortcomings of the NYT viewpoint here) (Solis 2009), the emerging view of audience measures for Twitter is to calculate the Followers of each person tweeting about the subject of interest, and then adding Follower numbers for each person retweeting the subject and so on. The issue here, much as it is in traditional public relations, is that the audience figure that results from these sorts of calculations grossly overstates, by one or two orders of magnitude or more, the actual "audience" for these tweets. It is a hypothetical number that assumes everyone that possibly could see a tweet has in fact seen it, and everyone who sees it is relevant to you/your brand. This is fantasy of course.

On the issue of relevant audience, here is a quick example. At the time I pulled these figures, the audited circulation of the *New York Times* was 4,974,000. Most public relations professionals getting a "hit" in the NYT would claim this as their audience. However:

- If you were only trying to reach a C-Suite audience with your message, the actual audience reached would be 598,000 or 12 percent of the total circulation;
- If you were trying to reach women, your audience would be 1,937,000 or 39 percent of the total; and
- If you were trying to reach 25- to 54-year-old men, your potential audience would have been 2,930,000, or 59 percent of the total number.

There is a large difference between how many people theoretically can see a tweet, versus how many actually saw it/read it, versus how many of those seeing the tweet find it relevant to them, versus how many engaged with it by hitting a link or retweeting. Part of my issue with this is the language we use to report the figures. For the Brew staff to use these numbers to estimate 1.43 million people "had seen tweets about it" is wrong. If they had said 1.43 million people had an opportunity to see the tweet, it would have been more realistic, although still greatly overstating actual relevant audience.

This problem of audience inflation has already been institutionalized in public relations. The use of Impressions as an output metric does not mean a true impression in the branding sense, but rather an opportunity to see the content. To make matters worse, many public relations professionals believe that Impressions should be factored by either dubious pass-along readership figures and/or use of a multiplier to account for the mythical credibility advantage public relations enjoys over impressions generated from advertising. The simple fact is that there is no research-supported, fact-based argument for using any adder or multiplier in public relations when calculating potential audience.

For Twitter and other social networks, we lack demographics and data about tweet readership averages (i.e., what is the probability that any one tweet is actually read) that would allow for more precise audience estimates. In the absence of data, believable assumptions should be used:

- Out of all the OTS, how many actually read the tweet? 10 percent?
- Of those reading the tweet, how many find it relevant to them (or from the other perspective, how many of the readers are in your intended target audience)? Maybe 10 percent again?

You can see how our audience estimate has already been reduced by a factor of 100. This may well still be overstating the actual, relevant audience. The issue here is that unrealistic and overstated audience figures have the potential to hurt credibility and call into question other data and metrics that may be more grounded in fact. Actually the more meaningful metrics pertain to engagement or outcomes rather than exposure/

outputs. It is more meaningful that 40,000 visited the Wordnik website as a result of the campaign discussed in the NYT article than the overstated 1.43 million who were estimated to have seen the tweets. The number 40,000 is real. One million forty-three thousand is fantasy.

A New Model for Social (and Traditional) Media Measurement

(August 29, 2008)

In November 2007 I suggested the current Outputs, Outtakes, Outcomes model and taxonomy for public relations measurement was confusing and therefore often misunderstood and misapplied (*more information in article "Let's put Outputs, Outtakes and Outcomes in the Outhouse" in Chapter 3*). At that time, I suggested that a simpler, more descriptive approach was in order and offered the following:

> What we need is a metrics taxonomy that is easier to understand and explain. Perhaps simple and descriptive enough that we could skip the need for explanation altogether. I propose the following three terms:
> - *Exposure*—to what degree have we created exposure to materials and message?
> - *Influence*—the degree to which exposure has influenced perceptions and attitudes.
> - *Action*—as a result of the public relations effort, what actions if any has the target taken?

Since November, I have given a lot of thought to the E–I–A construct and how to improve upon it. Some of the feedback to the model was that the gap between Exposure and Influence was too great, and perhaps there should be an interim step called Understanding or Relevance. There is also the social media dynamic to consider since the measurement model should be flexible enough to work for both traditional and social media.

What seems to fit best between Exposure and Influence, and adds richness to social media measurement, is the concept of *Engagement*. Not

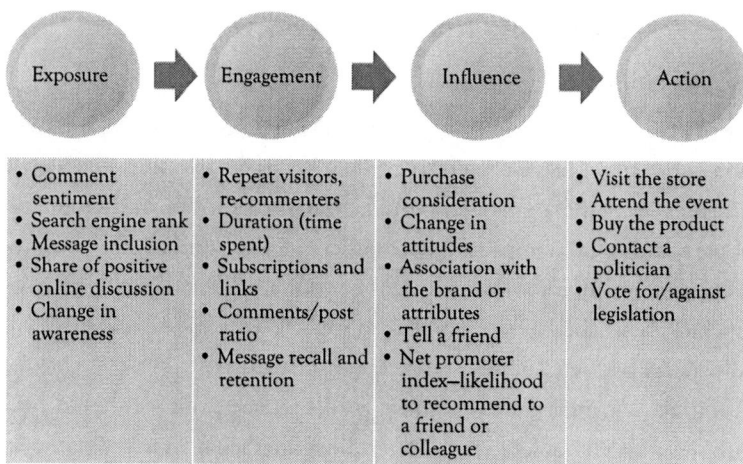

Figure 3.2 Exposure–engagement–influence–action model

only is it one of the hotter topics in social media, it is consistent with the desire to have more descriptive and easily understood metrics. With Engagement we now have a category that nicely contains such emerging key metrics as view-throughs, duration spent with content, repeat commenters, and comments to posts ratio. It also works well for old school metrics such as recall and retention. Engagement is what helps set the stage for Influence to occur. Engagement is necessary for communities to form. Engagement is fundamental to brand.

Figure 3.2 presents a graphic illustration that shows the new model and sample metrics that might be used at each stage.

I would love your feedback on this new Exposure→Engagement→ Influence→Action model.

There are still a few challenges in adoption of the model, not the least of which is that there is no consistent definition of Engagement. Current definitions range from the simple comments to post ratio used by *BusinessWeek* in their Reader Engagement Index, to the eight-term formula for Engagement offered by Eric T. Peterson (Peterson 2006). The next year should bring more clarity and consistency to our understanding and use of Engagement. At least there is modest agreement on the specific metrics contained within the category of Engagement.

Measuring Influence in Social Media

(June 4, 2009)

Every week there are multiple articles and posts on measuring Influence in social media. The vast majority of these focus on assessing who are the "Influencers"—those analysts, pundits, micro-celebrities, and visionaries whose words and actions influence others in their online communities. Influencers are an important element of your audience targeting strategy. In a blog post, Todd Defren explained well the concept of audiences and influencers (Defren 2009).

Influencers are a potential social media strategy, but we should measure social media objectives to determine whether or not programs are working as planned. For that we have to turn to the other type of online influence, *audience influence*.

With audience influence, we want to understand what influence, if any, our social media efforts have had on audience opinions, attitudes, and behaviors. Figure 3.3 presents a social media measurement model that shows where audience Influence fits with the other major measurement stages, Exposure, Engagement, and Action:

- *Exposure*—to what degree have we created exposure to content and message?
- *Engagement*—who, how, and where are people interacting/engaging with our content?
- *Influence*—the degree to which exposure and engagement have influenced perceptions and attitudes.
- *Action*—as a result of the social media effort, what actions if any has the target taken?

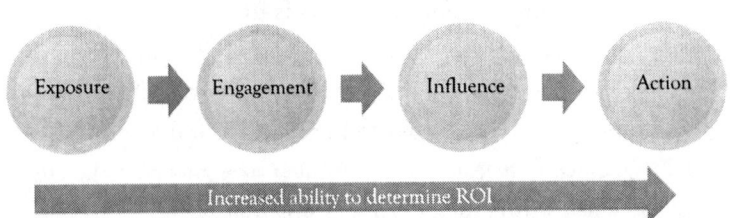

Figure 3.3 Influence's fit with exposure, engagement, and action

In the model, successful relationships with Influencers would be represented as an aspect of Engagement—that is, Influencers have the ability to influence if and how consumers engage with brands.

To measure audience influence typically requires primary research to quantify attitudes and opinions and to assess the role, if any, social media efforts had in any attitudinal changes and subsequent behavior. Once we understand how Exposure and Engagement are impacting Influence, and whether or not Influence is motivating Action, we are well on our way to the understanding and data necessary to demonstrate the true ROI generated by social media.

In summary, determining who has influence should be part of your audience targeting strategy; determining whether or not you are creating audience influence should be part of your measurement strategy.

Bringing Some Clarity to Social Media Influence

(December 10, 2011)

The emphasis on influencer marketing in social media has reached a fever pitch in 2011, and with it a flood of tools and opinions on how to navigate the influence waters. This is interesting in that one of the most powerful aspects of social media marketing is the ability to establish connections and relationships directly with prospects and customers and not have to go through an intermediary to communicate. But we'll leave that to the social strategists to reconcile and justify. Influencer marketing is hardly a new strategy. Through the years, much work in traditional public relations utilized influencer targeting (e.g., market analysts, financial analysts, key opinion leaders, other customers) to help amplify and endorse a brand or a company's products and services. So why is there so much discussion and confusion about influence in social media? Let's explore.

Influence Basics

A definition I like for influence is *effecting change in another person's attitudes, opinions, beliefs, and/or behavior.* I believe the most overlooked word in this definition is *change.* Without change influence has not truly occurred. One challenge here is that influence can happen without any resulting short-term *observable* action. Influence takes hold primarily between the ears, not necessarily with hand on mouse or wallet. This creates fundamental challenges when trying to measure the degree to which influence has occurred.

Another challenge we face is that influence is contextual, not absolute. People who influence others do so primarily in areas where they have specific expertise or authority. It is common to be influential in one area but have little or no influence in others. One of the main issues with current influence tools is that they do a relatively poor job of establishing contextual relevance.

The distinction between creating influence within a target audience and who or what has influence over the target has a tendency to get muddled. To clarify, determining who has the potential to influence the target audience (the influencers) is a targeting question. Have we created influence (changed attitudes, opinions, beliefs, and/or behavior) is a measurement question.

Influence is purposeful. In real life or digital life, when we set out to change the opinion, attitude, beliefs, or behavior of another person or group, we do so with a downstream motivation—for them to take a specific action. The list of possible actions is lengthy—buy a product, visit a website, tell a friend, vote, wave a sign, and donate, to name a few. Of course, not all desired actions are equal in terms of the amount of influence required for change. Opinions might be easier to change than an attitude. An attitude is easier to change than a belief. Behavioral change can range from relatively easy to nearly impossible depending on the specific behavior. In marketing, the ultimate behavior or action we try to influence is purchase behavior. It is important to think through the specific actions you hope the target will take as a result of being influenced. This is also the sweet spot for influence measurement.

While creating an action/behavior change is the ultimate reason for influencing someone, it is helpful to think of the process of influence as two stages—opinion, attitude, or belief change—and then, because of this change, did an action occur or was a behavior changed. Stated another way, the opinion change is an intermediate or micro-outcome and the desired action is a final or macro-outcome. Depending on the type of purchase decision there may be a time lag between the micro- and macro-outcomes that make it difficult to connect the dots. In his book *The Business of Influence*, Philip Sheldrake presents a concept called the "Maturity of Influence Approach" (Sheldrake 2011). Basically it melds two important concepts to use when thinking about influence measurement—focus on the influence, not the influencer (Philip refers to this as "influence-centric"), and to start at the macro-outcome/action and trace the path of influence back to the source(s) of influence. One simple example of this in a B2B context would be to ask the prospect at the time they are ready to make a purchase, "What sources of information or opinion were most valuable to you in making your decision to buy our product?" A similar question or two can be asked using a pop-up survey in an e-commerce situation.

Influence and Engagement Confusion

A primary source of influence confusion is failing to distinguish between a simple act of engagement and the process of being influenced. If someone in my Twitter stream sends out a tweet and I retweet it, have they influenced me to retweet or have I simply engaged with that individual's content? Many who have written about social media influence have suggested that in retweeting the tweet, I have been influenced to do so. I do not believe that is the case. I have engaged with the content, but have there been any true changes in my attitudes, opinions, beliefs, or behavior? Again, the operative word here is *change*. Does the act of retweeting constitute a behavioral change? Probably not. Engagement—yes, influence—no.

Engagement is a necessary precondition to Influence. This social media measurement model (*more information in article "Measuring Influence in Social Media" in Chapter 3*) addresses the distinction. Without engagement you don't have the opportunity to influence. Influence, however, only occurs if that engagement leads to a change in attitudes, opinions, beliefs, and behavior.

Influence, Popularity, and Celebrity Confusion

There also seems to be some confusion about the difference between influence, popularity, and celebrity. Although related, and in some cases overlapping, they are three distinct concepts. In my opinion, at least some of the confusion stems from Klout and other influencer tools that seem to measure popularity but call it influence. So what is the difference?

- *Popularity* is the state of being popular—widely admired, accepted, or sought after.
- *Celebrity* is a famous person, renown, and fame.

If popularity is about being well-liked and celebrity is about being well-known, influence is more about being well-respected, with associations such as knowledge, persuasion, and trust. Some of the confusion lies in the fact that some celebrities do have influence over the types of behaviors that make the cash register ring. Oprah comes to mind. Other celebrities, while very popular, don't really have the ability to create meaningful influence. They can get content re-tweeted (*Winning!*) but do they have any influence over the types of actions that brands really value?

Keeping Online Influence in Perspective

As we discuss the intricacies of digital influence, we should also keep in mind the majority of influence that occurs in the analog world. I've seen estimates ranging from 70 to 90 percent of influence occurring by offline word-of-mouth. It's personal. It's about real family and friends and not Twitter friends. Influence is about a relatively small number of people (Dunbar's Number suggests that humans have a finite cognitive capacity to have around 150 social relationships with other humans) (Krotoski 2010), and not mass influence. The fact that most influence happens offline presents another significant measurement challenge.

In summary, I'll leave you with a few sound bites on social media influence:

- Influence is about change.
- Engagement leads to influence.
- One can be popular but not influential.
- Measure the influence not the influencer.
- Don't forget offline when measuring online influence.

A New Framework for Social Media Metrics and Measurement

(June 12, 2013)

Last week in Madrid, AMEC held their fifth European Summit on Measurement. This one was titled *Unlocking Business Performance— Communications Research and Analytics in Action*. One underlying premise of the program this year was that the time for talk is behind us and the time for action and putting into place the principles and practices of sound measurement is upon us. The later part of the program featured an update from the Director of Salience Insight Commercial, Mike Daniels, on social media standards including the recently published standardization effort from the cross-industry group called The Conclave, which may be found in *The Conclave Complete Social Media Measurement Standards June 2013* (The Conclave Social Media Measurement Standards 2013).

Once Mike discussed where we are with respect to standardization, Richard Bagnall (@richardbagnall), Chairman of the AMEC Social Media Measurement Group, and I as his vice-chair, presented a session on creating a new recommended framework for social media metrics and measurement. Essentially we tried to answer the question: "How do we take the standards work coming from The Conclave and operationalize it to create proper social media measurement?" Here is an overview of what we presented and what we are encouraging everyone to adopt and use. The framework templates, user guide, and a short video synopsis will be available for download from the AMEC website (AMEC 2013a), Social Media Measurement section, in the next week or so.

Valid Metrics Framework and Social Media

Our journey begins with the Valid Metrics Framework (see Figure 3.4), a measurement planning framework and template developed under the auspices of AMEC. The framework was designed to be flexible enough to address multiple aspects of public relations within a consistent measurement framework and approach.

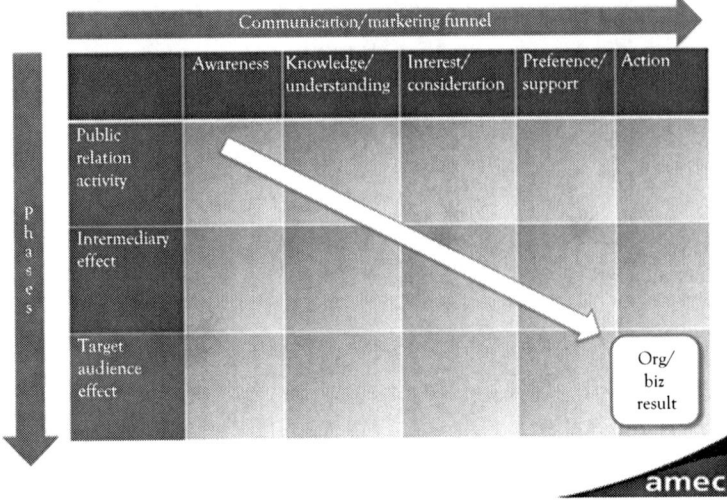

Figure 3.4 AMEC valid metrics framework

Note: Used with permission of AMEC.

Some of the most positive aspects of the Valid Metrics Framework are that it:

- provides a mechanism to link activities to outputs to outcomes;
- tracks through the familiar sales funnel; and
- helps create a focus on outcomes.

One of the applications of the Valid Metrics Framework was for use with social media programs. Two potential issues were surfaced by early adopters of the framework in social programs. The *intermediary effect*, which in traditional public relations is the impact on the media, seemed at odds with the social world of *direct interaction* between consumers and brands, and consumers with each other. And use of the marketing sales funnel (Court et al. 2009), while familiar, was only relevant in a percentage of social media use cases and perhaps not the best way to model common uses of social media such as customer relations and building relationships with stakeholder groups. Also, thought leaders such as Forrester Research and McKinsey & Company had noted that the traditional communication funnel was not necessarily funnel-shaped in social media. They described the discovery process that occurs when investigating companies and brands that often cause the consideration set to expand rather than be reduced, and the fact that a lot of engagement around brands happens post-conversion event. For all of these reasons our task was to develop and recommend a better framework and approach.

Models and Frameworks

When we use the word "model," we are referring to the representation of a system, in this case social media. In the original Valid Metrics Framework, the model used was the traditional sales funnel. A framework adds additional dimensions to the model and is operationalized with metrics. In the Valid Metrics Framework the additional dimensions are the phases—activities, intermediary effects, and target audience effects. We looked at both of these aspects individually and collectively when considering alternative approaches.

We studied and evaluated about 15 different social media and communication models. A couple of common patterns emerged. Several of the models, including Forrester's Customer Lifecycle (Forrester Research n.d.) and McKinsey's Customer Journey (Court et al. 2009), showed a post-purchase engagement/experience step. We judged this important to include in our recommended approach. And, we considered the importance of Engagement and Influence, as two key concepts in social media marketing and measurement; we decided to try to make these two elements explicit in our model as well.

Suggested Social Media Metrics Model

The model (see Figure 3.5) we developed is derivative of the categories chosen by The Conclave (Note: Richard Bagnall and I also participated in The Conclave) to organize social media metrics and definitions. We took a slightly different perspective on the front-end of the model and reordered the back-end to create this model for our new framework. The descriptions of the stages use the definitions from the smmstandrards.org work wherever possible.

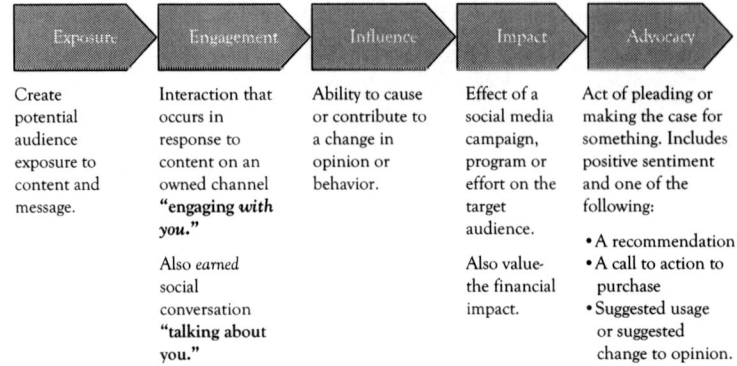

Exposure	Engagement	Influence	Impact	Advocacy
Create potential audience exposure to content and message.	Interaction that occurs in response to content on an owned channel "engaging *with you*." Also *earned* social conversation "talking about you."	Ability to cause or contribute to a change in opinion or behavior.	Effect of a social media campaign, program or effort on the target audience. Also value- the financial impact.	Act of pleading or making the case for something. Includes positive sentiment and one of the following: • A recommendation • A call to action to purchase • Suggested usage or suggested change to opinion.

Figure 3.5 Social media metrics model

Note: Used with permission of AMEC.

You will note that Engagement includes both interactions with owned social channels as well as earned social conversation of people "talking about you" in social channels. The definition of Influence is clear and concise, the result of a lot of discussion and prevailing clear thinking. The concept of Impact includes the outcomes of social initiatives as well as the Value those initiatives created. (I usually advise to always attempt to measure impact—and attribute value, when it is feasible and makes sense.) Advocacy includes a very helpful definition and conditions that exist with advocacy.

Creating the Framework

To create the framework, we explored various ways to address the "phases" of the Valid Metrics Framework. Two ideas stood out:

- Use a simple structure that captures social media metrics from three key perspectives—programmatic-level, channel-specific, and business. Programmatic metrics are those directly tied to social media objectives. Channel-specific metrics are just that, the metrics that are unique to specific social channels— tweets, retweets, Followers, Likes, Talking About This, Pins, Re-Pins. Business metrics are used to show the business impact of the campaign or initiative.
- Use Paid, Owned, and Earned media metrics for inte- grated programs containing these elements. Borrowing the

definitions from Forrester, Paid are social channels you pay to leverage (e.g., promoted tweets, display ads), Owned are channels you own and control (e.g., website, Facebook page), and Earned is where customers become the channel (e.g., word-of-mouth, viral).

There are certainly other ways to think about this (e.g., Business Performance Management [BPM]) and we intend to possibly add others based on industry feedback and suggestions.

The AMEC Social Media Valid Framework

Currently we have developed both versions with sample metrics (taken from the smmstandards.org work where applicable). We are calling them the AMEC Social Media Valid Framework. Table 3.1 is the version with program, channel, and business metrics shown.

Where Do We Go from Here?

Look for the completed frameworks on the AMEC website shortly. We encourage you to adopt the frameworks for use by your company or clients. If you like them and find them useful, please help promote them

Table 3.1 Sample metrics

	Exposure	Engagement	Influence	Impact	Advocacy
Program metrics	Total OTS for program content	Number of interactions with content Interaction rate Hashtag usage	Increased percentage associated with key attributes Change in issue sentiment	New subscribers Referral traffic to website White paper downloads	Recommendation to total mentions percentage
Channel metrics	Number of items Mentions Reach Impressions CPM	Post likes Comments Shares Views Retweets/1,000 Followers	Net promoter percentage by channel	Unique visitors to website referred from each channel	Organic posts by advocates Ratings/reviews
Business metrics			Purchase consideration percentage Likelihood to recommend percentage Association with brand attributes	Sales Repeat sales Purchase frequency Cost savings Number leads	Employee ambassadors Brad fans/advocates

Note: Used with permission of AMEC.

widely. And please provide your feedback on the proposed framework on this blog, or through the social channel of your choice. We're listening and looking forward to the dialogue.

New Framework for Social Media Measurement— Update and Debate

(June 21, 2013)

The complete presentation, including speaker notes, I gave at the AMEC Summit in Madrid on June 7 introducing the AMEC Social Media Valid Framework is now available for download from the AMEC website (AMEC 2013a). Please visit and download the slides if you are interested.

Whenever you throw a new idea or concept out there, you really hope that people see it. And you really, really hope they care enough about it to comment. Or better still, to challenge it and debate its merits. Simply put, critical thinking makes the concept better. Enter stage left, our provocateur, Philip Sheldrake (2011), author of *The Business of Influence*. Philip has also been an active thought leader in the whole push toward social media standards through AMEC committees and the work of The Conclave. I respect his opinion very much. Philip wrote a rather long essay on his blog (Sheldrake 2013) in response to my original post (*more information in article "A New Framework for Social Media Metrics and Measurement" in Chapter 3*) on the new Valid Framework for Social Media. Richard Bagnall, Chairman of the Social Media Measurement committee of AMEC, posted a response to some of Philip's concerns. I would like to address a few others now.

First, one area I am not going to address in this post is whether or not any framework for social media measurement should be driven by Business Performance Management (BPM) principles and approaches. That subject is being debated very well in the comments under Philip's original post—pretty interesting thread.

Stakeholders Versus Customers Versus Audiences

Philip questions if the framework, based on the words chosen to describe it, is oriented more toward customers (i.e., social media marketing) and not the broader concept of stakeholders. The intent was and is to make the framework broad enough to comprehend the majority of use cases for social media. Marketing is just one of the use cases (*more information in article "Social media ROI Part 2 Research Approaches" in Chapter 2*). To be fair, the use of "audience" in the description of Impact is a direct lift from the proposed standards document. We were trying to not reinvent the wheel. That said, I agree with you that saying stakeholders or publics is a more accurate description than "audience" in many cases.

Influence

It is hard to argue about influence with the guy who wrote a book on it, so I won't. Philip makes the point that the model offers a definition of influence ("Ability to cause or contribute to a change in opinion or behavior") but does not include the qualifying statements or concepts from the Word of Mouth Marketing Association (WOMMA) Guidebook—the potential to influence (before) and the actual, observed influence (during/after). He goes on to say that he prefers emphasis on the second. I fully agree. The short definition was offered for clarity and brevity. We will plan to reword this slightly to broaden. You'll note that the illustrative metrics shown in the framework with metrics are consistent with the during/after (e.g., change in purchase consideration) rather than before orientation. If you think about it, the before piece is really about targeting (who are the influencers we should engage?) rather than measurement (did we change opinion, attitudes, or behavior of our target stakeholders?).

Value

Philip makes the point that in the model's verbiage, the only reference to Value was financial impact whilst the standards definition reads, "the importance, worth or usefulness of something." Philip also acknowledges that this definition was a "last minute tweak." It was actually being debated as the slides were being developed. We'll broaden the definition to include tangible and intangible value to be in lock-step with the standards document.

Advocacy

Philip poses two great questions regarding this phase. His first point is a "good" model that includes advocacy should also be able to comprehend opposition and advocacy for competing agendas. I fully agree that these are important to consider and the model certainly does not preclude that. Comprehending these factors would be addressed by one or more metrics within the framework (e.g., Net Positive Advocacy—positive minus negative advocacy) or simply as a point of analysis rather than measurement per se.

Philip's second question is simply why Advocacy is shown after Impact. It is shown in this order to recognize the fact that most advocacy actually occurs post-impact or conversion event. For example, in a sales context, advocacy generally occurs after someone has bought and had great experiences with the product or service. To be more accurate, we might also show Advocacy after Influence and before Impact. Certainly issue advocacy often happens as a direct outcome of a change in opinion or attitude. Rather than show it in two places, to keep it simple, we choose to show it in the sequence where it is most relevant. In practice you could have both pre- and post-impact advocacy metrics in your measurement plan.

Paid, Owned, Earned

Philip simply questions the strategic value of this taxonomy and says it props-up organizational silos and reinforces misconceptions such as public relations equals (only) earned media. I think the questions are valid ones. But as a practical matter many companies and organizations do use the taxonomy. That is a key reason why it is one of the framework alternatives. And while it can reinforce silos and misperceptions, I have actually seen it have the opposite impact—it recognizes that integrated programs require integrated measurement and bring three key elements (different departments and sometimes different agencies) together under a common framework. Interestingly in public relations, we now routinely develop programs that include earned, paid, and owned elements. This reinforces the positive perception that public relations today is not simply equal to earned media.

Impact

Finally, Philip questions whether any framework can consider programmatic-level or channel-specific metrics in terms of Impact. I think it can and does. Impact refers to outcomes. We can have macro- and microconversions. And we can have outcomes that are specific to programs (e.g., event attendance, voter registrations, and subscriptions to a content series) or channels (download a whitepaper from the website), although I will agree that there will be few channel-specific outcomes.

Let's keep in mind that the metrics shown in the frameworks are illustrative, as Richard pointed out in his remarks, they are not meant to be exhaustive, definitive, or recommended. They are illustrative of the emerging standard metrics for social media.

CHAPTER 4

The "Tail" and the "Dog" in Social Media Measurement

Don's contribution to the body of knowledge on all things measurement has left its mark, his understanding in social media has helped to shape approaches to measurement in that space, and he was valued by us all not only for his smarts but also his humor, his smile, his company at various events, and in so many other ways—we all have our stories to tell.

—Pauline Draper-Watts, Executive Vice President at Edelman Intelligence, Global Lead—Measurement and Analytics

This chapter includes:

- The use of social media measurement listening tools in research and measurement
- Best practices in selecting a social media measurement vendor
- The planning–selecting–deploying process for social media listening platforms

Don't Let the Tool Tail Wag the Measurement Dog

(June 19, 2010)

Social media listening and measurement tools are sexy. Well, at least to those of us in research and measurement—it's all relative right? In the last three years or so there has been an explosion of social media tool vendors and platform choices. Tools are sexy and important, but in the grand scheme of things they are being overemphasized to some degree. We are letting tools decide what we can measure without giving sufficient thought to what we should measure. We are letting the tool tail wag the measurement dog.

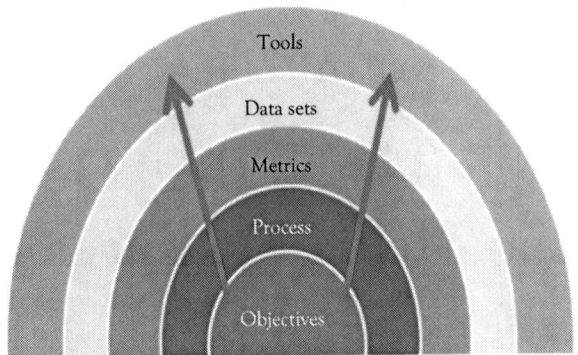

Figure 4.1 The decision process

There are several steps and decisions that should be addressed prior to selecting a tool or suite of tools. Consider Figure 4.1 as a starting point to help you think through these interim considerations and decisions.

Objectives

Proper social media objectives should be measurable (indicate change in metric of interest and time frame) and aligned with desired organizational outcomes. Understanding the social media objectives will suggest broad parameters of the measurement program, and ultimately the tool decision, must operate within. For example, geographic coverage requirements, type of content to be considered, and on-platform engagement capability may all be strongly suggested, based on a review of social media objectives.

Process

In addition to comprehending organizational or business outcomes, it is essential to understand the business process that the social media program will address or drive. If the program is marketing-oriented, the sales funnel process (Awareness/Consideration/Preference/Sales/Loyalty) may be most appropriate. For a brand-building campaign, the brand pyramid (Presence/Relevance/Performance/Advantage/Bonding) is what you want to measure your program impact against. Other business processes that are commonly addressed by social media programs include customer service and support, customer relationship management (CRM), corporate reputation, and lead generation.

Metrics

Understanding the requisite business process that the social media program is driving is crucial because each business process drives specific metrics. For example, the sales funnel drives a specific metrics set: percentage of unaided or aided awareness; percentage of the target audience who would consider the product/company; percentage who prefer the product/company; incremental sales revenues; percentage who would purchase the product again, number, or the number/amount of repeat purchases. For business-to-business (B2B) companies, the lead generation process would drive a different set of metrics: number of incoming leads; percentage/number of qualified leads; lead conversion rate; sales revenues generated. In addition to the business process metric sets, there are other metrics areas such as Exposure and Engagement we will want to address. Reach/opportunities to see, share of positive discussion, comments to post ratio, number of @ mentions and retweets (RTs) per 1,000 followers are examples of "standard" metrics that might be applicable for many social media programs.

Understanding how the social media program drives a specific business process is also important to our ability to describe the impact or, in some cases, return on investment (ROI) the program has created.

Data Sets

Each metric has data requirements, usually two pieces of data per metric—a numerator and a denominator. Examine the set of metrics you have defined for your social media program. Catalog all the specific pieces of data you need to compute the various metrics. For example, the data needed to compute the basic sales funnel metrics and some "standard" metrics might include:

- Number of individuals in the target audience
- Number of survey respondents
- Number of respondents "aware" of the product/company
- Number of respondents who would consider/seriously consider purchasing the product/doing business with the company
- Number of respondents purchasing the product
- Amount of sales revenue directly attributable to the program
- Number of purchasers who purchased again
- Total branded mentions
- Volume of positive and negative mentions
- Number of posts
- Number of comments
- Number of RTs and @ mentions
- Number of followers
- *Tools*

Armed with an understanding of all the data needed to calculate the metrics required to measure the social media program, you will be able to assess which tools or classes of tools best deliver the data you need. Pick the best three to five tools for further evaluation. You most likely will find that no one tool can deliver the complete data set you need. It is common to need two or more tools (e.g., web analytics package and social content analysis platform) in order to fully meet data requirements. Budgetary constraints may also limit your ability to capture the entire data set required.

By addressing the interim steps leading up to tool selection, you will be able to make a more informed tool decision. You also will have a much better chance of measuring what you should measure rather than settling for what you can measure. No tool before its time. Let the big dogs run.

Social Media Haiku

(March 26, 2009)
A little silliness for a Thursday afternoon … compiled from my Twitter series.

Good Is Never Easy
Social Media
Is Not Easily Measured
But We Must All Try.
Engagement Not Eyeballs
Engagement Is Key
But How to Best Measure It?
Not by Counting Clips!
Trust Me, It Works
Social Media
ROI Not Understood
Just Trust It's Working?

Ten Important Considerations When Selecting a Social Media Measurement Vendor

(July 1, 2008)

The majority of conversation today within the measurement community pertains to social media measurement. And the number of firms offering tracking, monitoring, or social media measurement solutions is exploding, doubling or more from 2007 to 2008. So, how do you select a firm that best meets your needs or the needs of your clients? Here are 10 items to consider as you start down that path.

1. *Underlying philosophy and capabilities*—There are many different approaches and underlying philosophies driving the various social media measurement vendors. Some of the approaches translate directly into unique capabilities. For example, CoreX, a company focused on defensive monitoring, is driven by a belief that participating in a discussion may unintentionally influence its outcome. Therefore, your identity is hidden when you use the tool. Compete tracks a consumer's online behavior/clicks while most other vendors track consumer artifacts such as comments or posts. Kaava focuses on communities and not blogs and believes that they better represent consumer opinion. Pick a partner with a philosophy that is compatible with your own views and needs.

2. *Metrics and analytics*—Give some thought to the specific metrics you want to track and the analytics that will give you the best data upon which to make decisions. While most firms track basic metrics such as volume of posts or comments and number of links, more complex or algorithmic metrics vary widely. There are many different interpretations of Influence for example. Also evaluate the range of analytics that are available. If links analysis or social network analysis is important to you, some social media vendors offer these while others do not. The good news is that the analytics and visualization tools available are rapidly becoming more sophisticated and useful.

3. *Content*—It is important to understand how content is brought into the social media measurement site, and how many different sources are looked at in order to find relevant content. Some sites claim 10 million sources while others claim 30 million. You also want to ensure that the sites trolled are the "right" ones for you or your clients. Develop a list of your 100 most important sites and ask the prospective vendor to verify whether or not each of the 100 is included in their universe of content. Also note which categories of content are tracked—discussion groups, blogs, review sites, traditional online media outlets, and so forth.

4. *Language support*—Are you most interested in the United States, Europe, or perhaps China? How you answer may well lead you to consider an entirely different set of vendor alternatives. If Europe is most important to you, you might consider a European specialist such as London-based Attentio, or perhaps Onalytica. If you are most interested in social media conversations in China, you might consider a vendor such as CIC that offers a deep understanding of Chinese pop culture and works in Shanghainese, as well as Mandarin and Cantonese. Just offering language translation is vastly easier than understanding cultural nuances of language usage within a given country. If your requirements are global, either make sure your analysis partner supports the languages that are important to you, or select two or three regional partners that collectively can support your global requirements.

5. *Real-time orientation*—Do you need information for crisis or issues monitoring or perhaps investing (*Collective Intellect*)? If so, you will need a vendor who provides near real-time updates of information.

The search-orientation model offered by many vendors is more akin to batch processing. You define terms you are interested in and then bots go and gather the information for your review and analysis. If crisis or issues monitoring is your primary requirement, make sure your vendor also offers capabilities such as e-mail or phone alerts.

6. *SaaS (software-as-a-service) or Consultative models*—Do you want a platform to do your own social media monitoring or do you want a firm to do the research and prepare a monthly report for you? Hands-on or hands-off? Some vendors (BuzzLogic, NetMap Analytics, Radian 6, and Visible Technologies to name a few) offer a SaaS model, while at the other end of the spectrum, others (MotiveQuest) are very oriented toward consulting—helping to answer the "so what should we do about it" question. Most of the firms offering a SaaS use a dashboard as their main interface. If creating dashboards for reports and/or having a dashboard interface is important to you, make sure to ask whether or not this capability exists and have it demonstrated to you to assess the overall ease-of-use and utility.

7. *Automated or Human analysis*—One of the ongoing controversies in the measurement field is what can be successfully automated in content analysis and what must or should be left to human analysis. A few vendors, Umbria for example, are fully automated, even for sentiment analysis. The majority of social media measurement vendors employ a hybrid approach, with simple items such as post or comment counts and number of links fully automated, but sentiment analysis left to human analysis. Some vendors perform the sentiment analysis while others leave the user to define sentiment for themselves.

8. *Ability to directly engage with consumers*—Some monitoring and analysis vendors allow you to directly engage in consumer discussion without leaving their platform. Visible Technologies and Digital Influence Group are two examples. This may be advantageous in situations where you are attempting to "Listen and Engage," rather than just measure online conversations.

9. *Customizability*—As you look at specific vendors and the tools and metrics they offer, you would be wise to ask whether or not any of the approaches, content sources, metrics, or algorithms can be altered to better meet your needs. For example, if specific social media sites

are critical to you, make sure they are being included in the content population. Filtering capability allows you to exclude sources you may not want to consider. Some tools, such as Radian 6 for example, allow the user to customize (via a graphic equalizer-like interface) the weighting given to specific elements when calculating Influence. You can put more of less emphasis on elements such as Number of On-topic Posts or Number of Links to better fit your own definition of online Influence.

10. *Cost*—Costs vary greatly, driven by many of the factors above. Obviously human analysis and consulting are major cost drivers. Tools range from free (always a strong price point!) to $1,000–2,000 a month, to $100,000 or more per year. Decide what you can reasonably spend before you do too much vendor analysis. For example, there is no sense in looking at vendors oriented toward consulting if you have only $1,000 per month to spend.

There are many additional factors you may want to consider when comparing firms. Number of years in business, clients/customers they do business with, and their ownership structure to name a few. I hope you will find the ten considerations presented useful as you try to find the best social media analysis for you. Happy hunting![1]

A 30,000-Foot View of Social Media Measurement

(July 2, 2009)

Look back five years and the public relations measurement field was full of challenges:

- Emphasis on media relations at the exclusion of other high-value public relations activities, almost always

---

[1] For more complete information to help you select the right social media measurement company, please visit Social Target (www.socialtarget.com). Founder Nathan Gilliatt produces the industry's best reference guide of social media analysis vendor information. Disclaimer—My employer's parent company, IPG, has a nonexclusive agreement with Radian 6.

- Oriented toward outputs and not outcomes, consisting
- Primarily of media content analysis, with
- Little primary audience research, and
- No codified thinking on how to approach ROI determination.

Now add social media. Old metrics such as Impressions lose meaning. It's about engagement and not eyeballs. Consumers have broad platforms to voice opinions about your brand. *Conversations* are more effective than *messages.* So needless to say, social media measurement is a highly fluid, and rapidly evolving field. Lots of opinions, not much consensus. Here is where I believe we are at a high level.

Early efforts to measure digital and social media focused almost exclusively on web analytics. I would say that the majority (80 percent?) of social media measurement in 2009 still focuses on web analytics, although many other forms of data and research are being used by leading organizations and professionals.

Today, the frontier in social media measurement is evolving toward measuring the conversations and behavior patterns occurring within social networks. The third area of interest is in tracking and connecting online and offline behavior and actions. Figure 4.2 presents a simple graphic (you may have a much better way of showing this) that shows these three primary interest areas, or zones, for social media measurement.

From the left, companies or brands control, own, or manage websites—corporate sites, Facebook pages, Twitter accounts, LinkedIn pages, and blogs by way of example—and create content that consumers may engage with. This zone is measured primarily by web analytics. In the middle are the actual social networks and conversations between individuals. In this zone we are interested in data sets that cannot be gathered

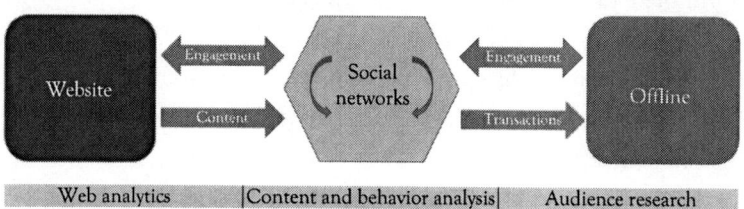

Figure 4.2 Social media measurement zones

solely using web analytics packages. How often is the brand being mentioned in conversation? What is the sentiment of the comments? How often is the brand being recommended and by whom? Content and behavior analysis, including tracking technologies, are the primary measurement tools in this zone. The third zone represents all the real-world, offline transactions that may be of interest. Did someone visit the store or attend an event? Did they buy a product? Did they recommend the brand or product to a friend over coffee? Primary audience research is necessary to address many of the questions, as well as scan or other purchase data in some cases.

Although I have attempted to define three distinct zones of measurement necessary to address the full spectrum of social media impact and ROI, your measurement strategy should be to take a holistic, integrated approach using methodologies, tools, and data from all three zones. The Holy Grail in many ways is to be able to track behavior of individuals across all three zones, cross-platform, understanding how online behavior impacts offline behavior and vice versa. It won't take five years to get there.

Twitter Influence Tools: Beware of Shiny Objects!

(November 18, 2009)

The proliferation of Twitter analytics tools continues. One of the most popular categories are tools that purport to calculate Twitter influence, that is, identify the individuals who influence others. They go by clever names—Tweetlevel, Twinfluence, and Twittergrader to mention a few. Brian Solis (2008) has provided a good list of Twitter tools. They are fun—who doesn't want to punch in their Twitter user name and see how "influential" you are? But are they truly useful? Should anyone base serious marketing or business decisions on these tools?

All these tools take a similar conceptual approach:

1. Define the terms that are believed to be related to Influence.
2. Arrange the terms in a sophisticated-looking formula. Better yet—call it an *algorithm*.
3. Factor the terms of the formula according to some proprietary coefficient weighting. (Tip: Labeling them "proprietary" heightens the perception of mathematical precision.)

4. Add a lot of terms to the formula so it seems complicated to the casual observer. (Tip: Complexity will heighten believability. Make it too understandable and believability may suffer.)

The game here is to create an aura of rigor *when one in fact does not exist.*

Equations Are Easy, Coefficients Are Hard

I suspect that in all the models discussed or available, the critical weighting of variables—assigning beta coefficients—was done by judgment, not math.[2] To correctly assign coefficients, one would use statistical techniques involving means and standard deviations to determine the coefficient of each independent variable (number of followers, how often content is retweeted, etc.) and determine the relationships (correlation) to our dependent variable—Influence. The dependent variable should be observable and measurable. Here's where it further breaks down. The problem here is that no one is actually measuring *true* Influence—the ability of one individual to change another's opinions, attitudes, or behavior. You can't surmise whether or not an opinion or attitude has been impacted, you have to conduct research. Opinions and attitudes exist within individuals. You cannot assess this by proxy, looking strictly at online metrics. Online behavior can be measured without primary research, but offline behaviors have to be observed or reported.

Influence Is Contextual

Influence is contextual not absolute. An individual may have the ability to influence certain people in specific subject areas. Authority and trust are important constituent elements of influence. Do they have the authority to speak within a particular area and are their words and deeds trusted? The notion of coming up with an influence score without context is inherently flawed. It might be interesting, but it is not actionable.

---

[2] Editor: A beta coefficient is a statistic that provides information as to the slope of a line in a regression equation. There are standardized betas (β) and unstandardized β.

According to the results generated by this class of tools, I believe they are probably assessing *popularity* much more than Influence in a meaningful way. According to Tweetlevel this morning, Ashton Kutcher is the second-most influential person on Twitter. Who exactly does he influence and in which areas? Mr. Kutcher is popular (number one in popularity) but I'm skeptical of his true influence. He is also the most trusted person on Twitter according to Tweetlevel. The second-most trusted person—Perez Hilton. Enough said.

Marketing Not Math

While I have been critical of these tools, I am not naïve enough to believe that the intent was to create a rigorous analytic tool that could be used to target individuals who might have the most influence over your target customers. These tools are most likely designed to put a hand on your wallet, not insights in your marketing effort. Do they work for marketing purposes? It is hard to say, but I'm sure they do in some cases. But, proceed with caution. You are walking a slippery slope in my view if you believe that developing a pseudo algorithm and slick website is the best indication that a company has the digital chops and experience to help drive your social business efforts. Getting to know the individuals involved and the work they have performed for companies like yours is preferable. Beware of shiny objects, they are not always as they seem.

Social Media Measurement 2011: Five Things to Forget and Five Things to Learn

(December 30, 2010)

It has been said that social media came of age in 2010. Not so for social media measurement. But the mainstreaming of social media marketing brings with it a heightened call for accountability. The need to prove the value of social media initiatives has never been greater. So, perhaps 2011 will be the year that social media measurement matures and comes of age.

As we look to the next year, here are five things to forget and five things to learn about social media measurement in 2011.

Things to Forget in 2011

1. *Impressions*

   The public relations industry has historically measured and reported success through the lens of quantity not quality. The most common public relations metric today is Impressions. While it is a somewhat dubious metric for traditional media, it really loses meaning in social media where engagement not eyeballs is what we seek. Impressions also (greatly) overstate actual relevant audience. Impressions merely represent an opportunity to see; they do not attempt to estimate the (small) percentage of the potential audience that actually saw your content.

   For Twitter, many folks use the sum of all first-generation followers as "impressions" for a particular tweet. The obvious problem here is that the probability that any one follower sees any one tweet is quite small. I don't have good data on this (please share if you do), but an educated guess might put the percentage at less than 5 percent. Similarly, for Facebook, use of impressions as a metric is also problematic. Facebook impressions do not indicate unique reach and you don't have any idea who, if anyone, actually viewed the content.

   Number of Impressions is a flawed, unwashed masses metric for social media measurement. Any time you are tempted to use the word "impressions" in social media, think about "potential reach" or "opportunities to see" instead. Or better yet, concentrate on Engagement and Influence.

2. *Vanity metrics—fans and followers*

   Most social media measurement efforts place far too much emphasis on Fans/Likers and Followers. For Twitter, the number of Followers is seen as a key metric, thought by many to relate to potential influence. For Facebook it is the number of Fans/Likers many companies/brands attempt to maximize. While these may be the vanity metrics of choice, they fall far short of being adequate for rigorous measurement. The largest disconnect of course is these numbers really don't describe potential audience size very well and they have nothing to do with interactions/engagement.

For Twitter, there is a growing amount of evidence (read the "Million Follower Fallacy" article) that number of Followers really has little to do with Influence (Cha et al. 2010). Number of Followers may be an indication of popularity but not influence. Influence talks more to one's ability to start conversations and spread ideas. For Facebook, number of Fans bears little semblance to average daily audience size and tells you nothing about engagement of the community. All Fans are not created equally. Some are engaged; some never return. Some are your best customers; others are there only to trash you.

Number of Fans and Followers are metrics you probably should include in your overall metrics set, but should be de-emphasized and not be a primary area of focus.

3. *Standardization*

Measurement standardization is always an interesting topic to debate. On one side you have the folks who believe that standards are absolutely necessary for measurement to proliferate, and on the other side you have the snowflake measurement disciples who believe that each program is unique and therefore requires unique objectives/metrics. I fall somewhere between the two extremes.

In June 2010 IPR, AMEC, PRSA, ICCO (International Communications Consultancy Organization), and The Global Alliance got together in Barcelona for a conference intended to create an atmosphere for measurement consistency/standardization around a codified set of principles of good measurement. The *Barcelona Principles* as they have come to be called are basic statements of good measurement practice—focus on outcomes not outputs, don't use advertising value equivalents (AVEs), and so forth. There is absolutely nothing to disagree with in the *Principles*. However, the heavy lifting of standardization comes at the metricslevel. Subcommittees have been formed that are taking the *Principles* all the way down to the metrics level. I have reviewed the work of the social media committee and believe that there is a lot of good work being done.

But in 2011, I expect a lot of debate but not a lot of progress in creating social media measurement standardization. One to watch is the Klout score for online influencers, which is being integrated as metadata in social media listening and engagement platforms. There are issues with the Klout score (for more information, read the blog post on *Bright Matrices* by Zavarello 2010) and I question the type of "influence" it is measuring—there is a big difference between motivating someone to action (e.g., retweeting your content) and motivating someone to purchase, which is ultimately the type of influence many companies and brands are most interested in effecting.

4. *Ad or media equivalency*

One of the truly insidious aspects of public relations measurement is the use of advertising or media equivalency (AVEs—advertising value equivalency) to assign financial value to public relations outputs. It is a highly flawed, path of least resistance attempt to calculate ROI for public relations. There are many reasons why using ad equivalency as a proxy for public relations value is not advisable.

To make matters worse, the practice has clearly moved into social media measurement as well. For example, research studies that monetize the value of a Facebook Fan/Liker by attributing an arbitrary \$5 CPM[3] value from the advertising world. Online media impact rankings also utilize equivalent paid advertising value to assign monetary value to online news and social media. The true value of social media is not how much an equivalent ad would have cost but in the impact it has on brand, reputation, and marketing.

5. *Return on engagement/influence/and so on*

Not a day goes by without someone declaring a new and improved metric for the acronym ROI, or stating that ROI does not apply in social networks. A recent Google search for "Return on Engagement" returned 192,000 results. "Return on Influence" returned 68,300.

Most of the folks who use these terms either don't understand ROI or don't know how to obtain the data necessary to calculate it. Many confuse the notion of impact with ROI (addressed in Things to Learn, below). Engagement creates impact for a brand or

---

[3] Editor: CPM means "Cost per Mille," which means cost per 1,000 impressions.

organization, but may or may not generate ROI in the short term. Creating influence—effecting someone's attitudes, opinions, and/or actions—creates impact but may or may not create ROI in the short term. It is often better to think about measuring impact first and then deciding whether or not you have the means and data necessary to attribute financial value.

Things to Learn in 2011

1. *Measurable objectives*
   There are many issues and challenges in the field of social media measurement. The easiest one to fix is for everybody to learn how to *write measurable objectives*. Most objectives today are either not measurable as written or are strategies masquerading as objectives (e.g., any sentence starting with an action buzzword such as "leverage" is a strategy).

   "Increase awareness of product X" is not a measurable objective. In order to be measurable, objectives must contain two essential elements:
   - Must indicate change in metric of interest—from X to Y.
   - Must indicate a time frame for the desired change—weeks, months, quarter, year, specific dates tied to a campaign (pre/post).

   Therefore, properly stated, measurable objectives should look more like these:
   o   Increase awareness of product X from 23 to 50 percent by year-end 2011.
   o   Increase RTs per 1,000 Followers from 0.5 percent in Q1'11 to 10 percent by the end of Q2'11.

2. *Impact versus ROI*
   ROI is one of the most overused and misused terms in social media measurement. Many people say "ROI"; what they really just mean results or impact. ROI is a financial metric—percentage of dollars returned for a given investment/cost. The dollars may be revenue generated, dollars saved, or spending avoided. ROI is transactional.

ROI is a form of impact, but not all impact takes the form of ROI. Impact is created when people become aware of us; engage with our content or brand ambassadors; are influenced by engagement with content or other people; or take some action such as recommending to a friend, writing a review, or buying a product. Impact ultimately creates value for an organization, but the value creation occurs over time, not at a point in time. Value creation is process-oriented. It has both tangible and intangible elements.

Your investments in social media or public relations remain an investment, creating additional value if done correctly, until which time they can be linked to a business outcome transaction that results in ROI.

Most social media initiatives today do not (or should not) have ROI as a primary objective. Most social programs are designed to create impact, not ROI, in the short term. There is also the notion that many social media initiatives are in an investment phase, not a return phase of maturity.

3. *Hypothetical ROI models*

One important step in determining how a social media initiative creates ROI for an organization is to create a hypothetical model that articulates the cascading logic steps in the process, as well as the data needed and assumptions used. The model is most useful in the planning stages of a program. It helps address the proverbial question, "If I approve this budget, what is a reasonable expectation for the results we will achieve?" Let's take a look at a simple Twitter example:

Program: Five promoted tweets are sent with a special offer to purchase a product on an e-commerce site.

Hypothetical ROI Model:

- (Data) Total potential unduplicated reach of the five tweets is 1,000,000 people.
- (Assume) 10 percent of the potential audience will actually see the tweet = 100,000 people.
- (Assume) 20 percent of the individuals who see the tweet find it relevant to them = 20,000 people.

- (Assume) 10 percent of those finding it relevant will visit the site = 2,000 people.
- (Assume) 10 percent of those visiting the site will convert and buy the product = 200 people.
- (Data) Incremental profit margin on each sale is $50.
- (Data) Total cost of the social media initiative is $2,400.

ROI Calculation: (200 × $50) = $10,000 – $2,400 = $7,600/ $2,400 = 3.17 × 100 = 317% ROI.

Our model suggests that this program will be successful and generate substantial ROI. If in reviewing a model with someone who needs to approve a program, they conceptually buy into the model but challenge its assumptions. *That is a positive step.* Negotiate different assumptions and rerun the numbers. Hypothetical models help you think through the data requirements your research approach must address in order to actually measure the ROI of the program after implementation.

4. *Integrated digital measurement*

The definition of public relations is fluid, and rapidly evolving to encompass a much broader and more integrated view of communications and how we connect, engage, and build relationships with consumers and other stakeholders. Digitization in all its forms has driven and accelerated this important change. Communicators should now take a more content and consumer-centric view of the world, orchestrating all the consumer touch points available in our increasingly digital world. At Fleishman–Hillard, we capture this expanded scope and integration in a model we refer to as PESO— Paid/Earned/Shared/Owned. Here is how we define the elements of our model:

- *Paid*—refers to all forms of paid content that exists on third-party channels or venues. This includes banner or display advertisements, pay-per-click programs, sponsorships, and advertorials.
- *Earned*—includes traditional media outreach as well as blogger relations/outreach where we attempt to influence and encourage third-party content providers to write about our clients, their products, and their services.

- *Shared*—refers to social networks and technologies controlled by consumers along with online and offline word-of-mouth (WOM).
- *Owned*—includes all websites and web properties controlled by a company or brand including company or product websites, micro-sites, blogs, Facebook pages, and Twitter channels.

The social media measurement Holy Grail in many ways is to be able to track behavior of individuals across platforms, online and offline, tethered and mobile, understanding how online behavior impacts offline behavior and vice versa. We also seek to understand how the PESO elements work together synergistically. For example, how exposure to online advertising impacts conversions within social channels. To address this, your measurement strategy should be to take a holistic, integrated approach using a variety of methodologies, tools, and data.

5. *Attribution*

If you are not already familiar with *value attribution models*, prepare to hear much more about them in 2011. Value attribution models attempt to assign a financial value to specific campaigns and/or channels (e.g., advertising, search, direct, social) that are part of a larger marketing effort. So rather than giving all the conversion credit to the last click in a chain or even the first click, the model attributes portions of the overall value across the relevant campaigns and/or channels.

A simple model might look at the following metrics for each channel:

- *Frequency*—the number of exposures to a specific marketing channel or campaign
- *Duration*—time on site for exposures referring to the conversion site
- *Recency*—credit for exposures ranging from first click to last click, with last click typically receiving more credit

Value attribution models require human analysis and expertise. This factor is often cited in studies as the reason more companies do not pursue attribution modeling.

Social Media Listening Platforms—Plan, Select, Deploy (Part One—Plan)

(May 19, 2011)

It is not difficult to find a social media listening platform/tool—there are over 100 to choose from. What is difficult is to find the *right* tool. It takes a keen understanding of your scope and requirements. It takes an evaluation and selection process that will surface the best platform to fully meet your requirements. And it takes a well thought-out process for deploying the platform across the organization in an effective and efficient manner. There are many questions to be asked and answers to be given. Asking the right questions at the right time is crucial.

It is helpful to think of the overall process in three phases:

- *Plan*—define requirements, stakeholders, and scope.
- *Select*—create a platform evaluation process tailored to your unique requirements.
- *Deploy*—the selected platform across the organization with training, workflow, and other important issues addressed.

This three-part series will tackle each phase one at a time. First up—Plan.

In many ways, the planning phase is the most important. Overlook an important detail here and you may or may not be able to overcome it later. Here are 10 topic areas to discuss within your organization to make sure you are setting yourself up for success.

1. *Stakeholders*—What are the primary stakeholder groups within my company or organization? Possible stakeholder groups might include marketing, corporate communications, and customer service/care at the macrolevel. Depending on the size of your organization, various regions, divisions, groups, or product lines may also be distinct stakeholder groups. Once you have identified the primary stakeholders, set up time to meet with each group. Understand how they currently use social listening tools and what, from their perspective, are "must have" capabilities versus "nice to have" capabilities in a social

listening platform. Ask each stakeholder group the applicable questions from the list below.

2. *Geographic scope*—What languages and countries are stakeholders interested in including in the platform? Try to understand the relative priority of each country and language. Also be sure to comprehend future requirements. For example, if Chinese is not a priority today but will be within two years, you may want to only consider listening platforms that support two-byte languages. Also probe to assess if social media content will need to be translated into other languages. This may be primarily an internal workflow issue or outsourcing issue, but might also be a platform consideration.

3. *Value-added services*—It is very important to develop a point of view on how monitoring, analysis, and reporting will be done within your organization. Will each stakeholder group be responsible for doing this themselves or will a centralized analytics and insights group be responsible? In addition to the self-serve approach, you could consider outsourcing this work to your social listening platform vendor or to one of your agencies—public relations, digital, or advertising. In my experience, it is easy for a company or organization to underestimate both the skill and time commitment necessary to make the self-serve approach effective.

4. *Content/Data types*—Social media listening platform vendors generally include content from the primary social media properties— Facebook, Twitter, Blogs, Forums, YouTube, and MySpace (being generous here). Flickr is also included in many. Currently on vendor roadmaps are properties such as LinkedIn and perhaps customer review sites. Make sure the content types the platform supports meet your stakeholder requirements. It is also very important to understand how the social content is being aggregated and how frequently (see Reporting, topic area 8, for more on latency issues). The fundamental ways in which content is aggregated in social listening platforms are crawling the web, RSS[4] feeds, and third-party content

---

[4] Editor: RSS stands for *Rich Site Summary* and can be used to monitor information from the Internet in a simpler and organized way.

aggregators (e.g., Boardreader for Forums). Many platform vendors employ a hybrid approach.

5. *Metrics and analytics*—Most social listening platforms either have a set group of analytics that deliver specific metrics or they offer configurable analytic "widgets" that may be used to create metrics such as share of conversation or volume and tone trend. Some platforms offer a combination of these two approaches. Based on your needs and measurement strategy/approach, define the analytics and metrics you would ideally like to see (e.g., volume, sentiment, messages, share-of-conversation, association with key topics). In the vendor selection phase, this list will be useful to compare and contrast vendors.

6. *Keywords and topics*—During the planning phase, it is wise to develop a list of the major keywords and topics that you believe will be necessary for the listening platform. These keywords might include the company name, key competitors, industry issues, market segment names, brand names, product names, key spokespersons, executives, and competitor and industry spokespersons. Social media listening platforms have varying degrees of sophistication with respect to their search capability. Some have full Boolean logic, others offer very simple *and/or* logic.[5] The importance of this difference depends to some degree on your company/brand name as well as the sophistication of the people who will be configuring and maintaining your system. If, for example, your company name is a common word (e.g., Apple, Visa), you will need stronger logic capabilities that include proximity search.

7. *Integration*—Integration of varying data types—search, web, social, advertising, customer opinion, and others—is the present and future

---

[5] Editor: Boolean logic allows for searches to be expanded or restricted. For instance, "and" will give you all references to two search categories while "not" will give you only those references that are not referring to. Examples: "public relations, measurement, AND advertising" will give you all the search findings for each of the terms; "public relations, advertising NOT measurement" would give you all the findings for advertising and public relations but not if they include "measurement."

of online measurement. It is therefore important to understand what capabilities, if any, the social listening platform vendor has to integrate with other data types/streams. Do they offer the ability to connect with web analytics packages via API[6] for example? The web/social integration is becoming increasingly common. If you need to integrate traditional media with social, it might be a nice feature if the social listening platform allows third-party content aggregators such as Factiva, Lexis Nexis, VMS, or Critical Mention.

8. *Reporting*—During the planning phase it is helpful to think through a series of questions about reports and reporting. What type of reports is necessary? Who will be responsible for their creation? How often will reports be issued? Does the system need the capability to automatically generate and deliver reports? What about automated alerts? There are quite a wide range of report capabilities represented by the various vendors in the listening space. One potentially critical area to explore during the vendor evaluation phase is related to report *frequency* and perhaps to report *type* (think crisis). That is how often new content is brought into the system. Content latency issues may cause real problems during a fast-moving crisis. Generally, the content latency differs by media type; best for Twitter and worst (perhaps) for forums, some of which restrict crawling to no more than once per day. Within Twitter, the type of relationship the vendor has with Twitter should also be explored. Not all Firehose arrangements are the same. While most social media listening platforms claim to be "real time," it is interesting to ask the vendors to define what they mean by "real time." The answers may surprise you.

9. *Access*—Discuss who needs access to the listening platform and what they want to see and be able to do once they are in the system. Do your different stakeholder groups (divisions, product lines, brands, corporate, marketing, and so forth) want or need a customized view of the data perhaps presented on a separate dashboard within the system? It is also a good idea to have a perspective on who your power

---

[6] Editor: API means Application Programming Interface, tools that are used for building software and applications.

users will be versus the casual users. This distinction applies not only to system access, but also in areas such as training.

10. *Engagement*—Some social media listening platforms support engagement with content owners directly from the platform, others do not. Some engagement capabilities are elegant, others are rudimentary. Make sure to explore the engagement needs of your stakeholders and understand how important this capability is to them in the short and long term. If engagement capabilities are important, you will also want to explore if the system allows users to tag content, assign content, manage assignments, and track workflow.

In Part Two, we'll examine a rigorous process for social media listening platform vendor evaluation and selection.

Social Media Listening Platforms—Plan, Select, Deploy (Part Two—Select)

(June 2, 2011)

In Part One, we discussed a range of topics designed to help you plan and define the scope and requirements for selecting and deploying a social media listening platform across your company or organization. In Part Two, we will use the knowledge and perspective we gained in planning to orchestrate a thorough and effective platform selection process.

Here is a scalable selection process that will help you surface and select the social media listening platform that best meets your unique situation and requirements.

1. *Define the individuals who will be involved in the selection process*—Inclusion is a powerful card to play here. Inclusion brings different perspectives together. Inclusion greatly improves chances for success when it is time to authorize purchase of a platform and get it deployed properly across the organization or company. Inclusion will increase the likelihood of acceptance and use of the platform across the organization. Include representatives from the major stakeholder groups identified during the planning process. You might include someone from your IT department. You might also include the

individuals who must authorize the purchase. A group of up to 10 is most workable. After 10 or so, I believe you will most likely experience diminishing returns on the incremental people added to the process.

2. *Develop a list of selection criteria organized by major category*—Based on the planning process we undertook in Part One, develop a list of categories that are most important to learn more about. Here are 10 categories you might consider including:

- *Content sources/Types and aggregation strategy*—What types of social content are brought into the system? How is the content aggregated (e.g., RSS, crawling, third-party aggregators)? How often is each type of content aggregated?
- *Data and search considerations*—How long is content archived, and is back data available? What data cleansing strategies are in place to address spam, splogs,[7] and duplicate content? Is full Boolean logic available for constructing searches?
- *Metrics and analytics*—What specific metrics are "standard" in the system? Is automated sentiment analysis offered at the brand or post level? What audience-level data is available?
- *Data presentation*—What dashboard features and functionality are offered? Can dashboards be customized by user or group? Are drill-down capabilities available for all analytics on the dashboard?
- *Engagement and workflow functionality*—Does the platform offer the ability to engage directly with content owners? Can "owned" content be managed on-platform? What workflow management and reporting capabilities are offered?
- *Integration*—What additional types of data may be integrated in the system—traditional media, web analytics, e-mail, call center, CRM, and so forth?
- *Reporting capability*—Does the platform have a report function? Can reports be customized? Automated?

---

[7] Editor: Splogs means spam blogs.

- *Geographic scope*—What countries and languages are addressed by the system? Are two-byte languages[8] supported?
- *Cost structure*—What is the cost basis—seat charge, subscription, content volume, and/or number of searches? How does pricing vary with increases in the cost basis?
- *Value-added services*—Does the listening platform vendor offer system configuration services? Do they perform analysis and reporting?

Within each major category, list the specific criteria most relevant and important to your requirements. For example, within the Data and Search Considerations category, you might list 10 specific criteria that you want to assess for each vendor:

- How often is Twitter data refreshed? Can refresh timing be specified?
- How often is new content from other sources crawled/brought into the system?
- How long can each content type be archived?
- Is back data available? How far back and at what cost?
- What data cleansing strategies are in place?
- Can data be easily exported in comma-separated values (CSV)/Excel format and is bulk data extraction supported?
- Can users build and customize topics and searches?
- What types of Boolean operators are supported?
- Is proximity search supported?
- Do users have the ability to date-range data for analysis?

3. *Develop a scorecard to use in evaluating the potential listening platform vendors/partners*—Using the major categories and specific criteria you have defined, develop an overall scorecard to be used in

---

[8] Editor: The difference between single-byte (one-byte) and double-byte (two-byte) languages lies in whether a language exceeds 256 characters. Languages that are based on Latin characters such as English, French, and German do not exceed 256 characters and are considered single-byte (one-byte) languages. Asian languages such as Chinese, Japanese, and Korean exceed the 256-character limit and require double-byte (two-byte) encoding, therefore are considered double-byte (two-byte) languages (Lionbridge 2013).

the evaluation process.[9] Think about creating a weighting system at the category level to help prioritize the importance of each category. Assign a number of points to each criteria within a given category. A scorecard might contain 10 categories each containing 10 criteria. Begin by assigning a one-point value to each criteria (100 points total) and then apply weighting at the category level.

4. *Develop the initial vendor consideration set*—List all the social media platform vendors you wish to consider. Pick ones you are familiar with and have positive experiences with as a starting point. Talk to colleagues within, and experts outside, the organization to gain their perspective on the platforms that should be considered. Read blog posts and reviews of the platforms to gain additional outside perspective. Visit vendor websites and watch demo videos. Pull it all together and gain consensus among your team on the platforms that will be considered.

5. *Do some homework and narrow the list to a manageable number (perhaps 5 to 10)*—If your initial vendor consideration set is too large (if it has more than 10 vendors it is too large), do some additional homework and narrow your list to a more manageable number.

6. *Develop and distribute a request for proposal (RFP) based on evaluation criteria*—Using the categories and criteria you developed, create a RFP, asking the listening platform vendors the questions that are most critical to meeting your requirements. Specify the format (e.g., PowerPoint, Word) you would like responses to take. Give the vendors about two weeks to respond.

7. *Evaluate and score vendor responses*—Once the RFP documents are received, each should be reviewed carefully and scored according to the criteria and weighting decided previously. Depending on the number of vendors being evaluated and ease of getting the entire

---

[9] Editor: A scorecard is a strategic management system that focuses on aligning and monitoring an organization against its strategic business goals and those of its competitors. Traditionally, this has been referred to as a "balanced scorecard" (Balanced Scorecard Institute 2009) with four components: financial, customer, internal business processes, and learning and growth. Any metric that provides *weights* to the various components (as many as desired) can be created.

evaluation team together, there may be merit in blocking out an afternoon to gather as a group, read through the responses, and decide how each will be scored. This is a bit of a "pulling off the band-aid" approach that will save time and allow for spirited discussion and consensus scoring. If this is impractical for whatever reason in your company or organization, assign one of more RFPs to individuals who will then develop the scorecards. The scorecards may then be reviewed together in a meeting or conference call, and consensus reached on scoring. Obviously the potential issue with multiple people independently creating scorecards is consistency. You want the evaluation to be as fair and consistent as possible, given whatever constraints you are working under.

8. *Develop a short list of vendors*—If your number of vendors under consideration is over five, use the scorecards to reduce the list to three to five platforms that will undergo further evaluation. These are your finalists. You should always promptly notify vendors not moving forward in the process, and offer to provide feedback via phone or e-mail on why they were not selected to move forward. This professionalism will be much appreciated by the vendors, and represents a good learning opportunity for all involved if done well.

9. *Deploy test scenarios*—At this point we have narrowed the list of contenders and are ready to proceed with some specific tests designed to illuminate the real-world capabilities of the platforms. Here are three possible test scenarios. You can use all three for a very rigorous evaluation, or just one or two if that fits your needs better.

- *Test Scenario 1*: Give each vendor a defined list of search terms (brands, competitors, issues) and the languages/countries you want to evaluate. You should use search terms that are directly relevant to your company or organization. Explain what type of analysis you would like performed and ask each to address insight generation. Platform vendors are given one week to prepare an analysis. If practical, you could ask each vendor to give a presentation of the results in person. Alternatively, use a web conference to review the results.

- *Test Scenario 2*: This is a real-time exercise designed to assess vendor data volume by country/language and signal-to-noise ratio of relevant content. Get on a web conference with each social media listening platform vendor. Give them a new list of three search terms and ask that they go into their platform, configure the system for the three search terms, and then pull in relevant content for the past 30 days. Once that is accomplished, ask them to export the data as a CSV or Excel file and e-mail you the results while everyone is still on the line. A more detailed off-line review of the results should be undertaken, including translation of languages, to assess relevancy of the results.

- *Test Scenario 3*: This has been referred to by a colleague as the "Dr. Evil test" … In conjunction with Test Scenario 2, it may be interesting to "plant" known content that matches the search terms on different Twitter channels, Facebook pages, and Forums in each country that is of interest to you. When you receive your data export, examine to determine if the known content was found.

10. *Pick a winner*—At this point you have the RFPs, scorecards, and test results. You are ready to make your decision. Convene the evaluation team, discuss the results, and make a decision. With luck, a clear winner will have emerged from the process. Contact the winner and negotiate terms of a contract. Don't notify the non-winners until after a contract is in place, just in case you need to move to your second choice for whatever reason.

In Part Three, we will discuss how to maximize your potential for success when actually deploying the social media listening platform across your organization.

Social Media Listening Platforms—Plan, Select, Deploy (Part Three—Deploy)

(June 17, 2011)

In Part Two of this series on social media listening platforms we offered a process for selecting a social media listening platform vendor. Now it's time to deploy the tool across your organization effectively and with minimal disruption. And put the tool to work.

Configuration

We talked about value-added services in the first post in this series. One of the services offered by many listening platform vendors is configuration. You'll have to decide if you want to have the vendor perform system configuration or do it yourself (DIY). In some cases, you have no choice—you submit keywords, topics, and themes to the vendor and the system is programmed for you. In other cases, some basic configuration must be done by the platform vendor but the bulk of the configuration can be a DIY project.

Keywords and Topics

In Part One of this series, we discussed the need to think through the keywords required to bring all relevant content into your platform. The keywords might be company name, product/brand names, competitors, issues, segment names, executives and spokespersons, and key messages. During deployment you will need to build taxonomy around many of the keywords that represent concepts rather than singular ideas or names. For example, if you have a message that centers on being an innovative company, you will have to decide what expressions in addition to the keyword "innovative" may be classified as innovation—leading-edge, technology leader, R&D leadership, breakthrough products, and so forth. You will also have to decide words and terms to *exclude* from your analysis. Both processes are iterative—make a change, check content relevancy, adjust, repeat.

Integration

There are a few different types of integration you may want to tackle during platform configuration and deployment. Each of the possible forms of integration will take a little time to accomplish and may require some back and forth between you and the platform vendor and/or vendor to vendor. I am a big fan of web analytics and social media integration. With many listening platforms this is relatively straightforward to accomplish. You may also want to integrate third-party data sources such as Factiva, LexisNexis, VMS, or Critical Mention. Assuming the listening platform vendor you selected supports this type of integration, it is relatively straightforward. To address latency issues, make sure you specify load times for the content.

Reports and Workflow

Previously, we addressed many of the basic questions around reports and reporting. In the deployment phase it's time to make it real. Design specific templates for each report you need. Create a mock-up and share with your stakeholders to make sure everyone is on board with the look, feel, and utility of the report. You will want to test the various delivery mechanisms to be employed including all e-mail clients and mobile platforms you believe may be used. Generally speaking, assume a significant percentage of the audience may look at the report on a mobile device, making this an especially important dynamic to test. Once you have the report format established, define your workflow process—who pulls data and when, who creates visuals and by when, who compiles and edits the report and by when, and who is responsible for distribution and against what schedule.

Training

The first decision to make with training is if you want to tackle it yourself or rely on the listening platform vendor to perform the training. Some vendors have very strong training programs and others not so much. Some vendors charge for training and some do the bulk of it for free. You most likely will want to take a train-the-trainer hybrid approach to training—have a core one/two/three people trained by the platform vendor, and then charge this team with training within your company or organization. With respect to training timing, make sure to begin training only after everyone has a log-in to the system so they can actually use the system during the training. I usually refer to this as "training with live ammo." If you don't do this, you'll find the half-life of training pretty short—folks forget most of what they have learned very rapidly. I also find a tell–show–do teaching methodology works very well (my friends at Radian 6 approach training this way). Show some slides that cover the basics, show a video or canned demo that brings it to life, and then have everyone do some hands-on exercises using the platform. Remember that you will need to address initial training needs as well as ongoing needs as new users are brought on the platform.

Event-Specific and Programmatic Planning

Related to keyword analysis and taxonomy build-out, it may be wise to create keyword groups for programs you know you will be asked to listen to and measure, and for any potential events, like a crisis, that you can anticipate or imagine. With respect to programmatic listening and measurement, generally a combination of the right keywords and date-ranging will allow you to pull in program-specific content. If programs are known at the time of configuration and deployment, get ahead of the curve and set-up the keyword groups or source filters you may need.

If a company, brand, or organization has a social listening program, you are remiss if you don't include specific keywords that may serve as an early-detection system for potential crisis. For example, depending on the type of organization and industry, it may be advisable to set up a keyword search like this: Company name AND fire OR explosion OR shooting OR recall OR kidnapping OR crash.

In today's real-time world, in my opinion, it is no longer optional to have social media listening capabilities. As a result of this three-part series on listening platforms, I hope you are better equipped to plan, select, and deploy your platform effectively.

CHAPTER 5

Getting a Robust and Effective Social Media Measurement Program

I first met Don at an Institute for Public Relations Measurement Commission meeting in New York City. Interestingly, Don knew who I was (we had three Dons on the Commission back then out of about 12 active members) and immediately engaged me in a conversation about research, measurement, and where it was to lead public relations to. I listened as he began to explain where he thought measurement was headed and for my benefit, how we should be retraining our public relations students in measurement. We continued that discussion for many years.

—Don W. Stacks, PhD, Professor of Public Relations and Corporate Communication, University of Miami

This chapter includes:

- The social media listening maturity model and how to evaluate your own practices
- The outlook of social media measurement

Three Fundamentals of Great Social Media Measurement

(February 20, 2012)

If you want to evaluate the robustness and effectiveness of your approach to social media measurement, ask yourself these three fundamental questions:

1. Does the approach measure the "right" things in order to show the business impact of the programs and initiatives?
2. Will stakeholders of the report receive the data and actionable insights required to make strategic decisions?
3. Are the data and insights presented in a clear and concise manner that tells a story and makes it easy to understand and act upon?

Measuring the "Right" Things

As demonstrated in Figure 5.1, social media metrics are derived from three primary sources.

Ideally, a robust social media measurement program will have a rich metrics set that contains metrics from all three areas. Metrics tied to program objectives allow for direct measurement of program success. Fundamentally, measurement is about assessing performance against objectives. It is surprising how often social program objectives are slanted toward channel-specific metrics (e.g., Likes or Followers) and not the specific outcomes desired for the program—what you hope to accomplish by implementing the program. Also, relying too heavily on channel metrics limits you to what you *can* measure rather than what you should measure. Business outcome metrics are used to connect the dots between

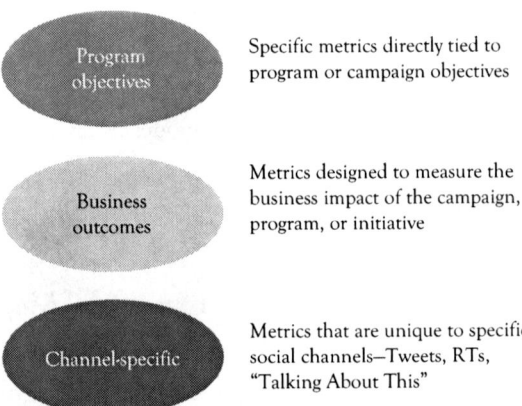

Figure 5.1 Social media metric sources

Note: Used with Permission of Ketchum.

social media programs and the business results they are designed to drive. Social programs that cannot answer, or at least address, the management question, "How is this impacting my business?," are more susceptible to resource allocation scrutiny (#pleasecutmybudget). Stated another way, if management asks how we're doing in social media and we reply, "Great, post virility is up 6.1 percent this month," we make it difficult for that individual to understand how social media/business initiatives are helping move the business forward.

Getting to Data and Insights That Inform Strategic Decisions

Expectations for social media measurement and analysis have risen. In addition to sound analysis and reporting of performance against key metrics and key performance indicators (KPIs), understanding audience dynamics, and developing actionable insights are rapidly becoming *de rigueur*. Insights may be defined as synthesizing and interpreting data to provide actionable information and knowledge that informs strategic decisions. Too many social media measurement programs take a social-centric rather than a business-centric approach to insights. They often feature insights and recommendations that are tactical in nature—the best time of day or how many times to tweet, or what type of content seems to be most successful. Ideally, insights and recommendations in social media measurement reports would be operating one level above this, informing strategic decisions about how social programs and conversations are impacting—or could impact—the business. To do this requires an understanding of the business function (e.g., marketing, customer service) impacted by the social program *and* an ability to ask the right questions prior to starting a social media analysis.

For example, let's say Company X plans to introduce a new video game. A social listening program has been implemented to analyze the early consumer reaction to the game. Based on the listening analysis, changes to the packaging, marketing, or even the product itself are possible. If you are in charge of the marketing campaign for the game, what are the types of social media insights you need to make decisions about the game and the marketing campaign?

- What is the level of buzz about the game? What is the overall sentiment? How does this compare to previous game launches?
- What are people talking about in social media—availability, cost, specific features of the game, packaging, marketing campaign?
- What features of the game do consumers seem to like most? Least? Specifically, what do they like or dislike?
- What are the most influential gaming enthusiasts saying about the product?
- Who are the promoters and detractors? What is the ratio of promoters to detractors? How does this compare to promoters and detractors from previous game launches?
- How much social media conversation contains recommendations or expresses purchase intent? How does this compare to previous launches?

Answering these types of questions provides actionable insights that provide context and can inform strategic marketing decisions.

Presenting Results

Dashboards have gotten a bit of a bad rap—not because dashboards are not useful, but because some have used them as *the* measurement report rather than just one aspect of a good report. I'm a dashboard proponent for a few reasons:

- Deciding which metrics to feature on a dashboard is a good strategic exercise requiring you to focus on the very most important and relevant metrics for the intended audience.
- Online, dynamic dashboards are an effective user interface that can be used as a launching-off point for drilling into data to understand the underlying story.
- Good dashboards present a snapshot of overall performance that is easily absorbed and understood.

A dashboard-driven social media measurement report is versatile and effective in many situations. A typical report might consist of one of more dashboards and then a deeper dive on each of the key metrics featured on the dashboards, along with audience insights, strategic insights, and recommendations. This format provides a quick snapshot (dashboard) of results, ideal for those stakeholders interested only in topline data, and provides sufficient depth to satisfy those more interested in the underlying drivers of the metric.

Social media measurement programs that are built around metrics tied to business outcomes and show how programs are performing against objectives are important. Reports that deliver clear insights that inform strategic decisions are important. And delivering those reports in a compelling format that enhances usability and effectiveness is important. How do your programs stack up?

Time to Get Real About Social Media Audience Reporting

(June 12, 2012)

Although almost everyone would agree that social media is about engagement and not eyeballs, too much of digital and social media measurement is focused on *audience size*. How many Followers do we have? How can we get a million Likes? How many unique visitors did we have to our site this month? And unfortunately, audience size estimates in social media grossly overstate the actual relevant audience. We seem fixated and oriented toward "how many," while our focus should be on "who" and specifically, "who within our target audience." Generally speaking, the advertising industry has led the way with audience measures and is ahead of where the public relations and social media camps are with respect to the level of sophistication.

In television advertising, the concept of Target Rating Points is a refinement of Gross Rating Points where you only measure and get "credit" for the percentage of the gross audience that meets your target audience criteria. In an effort to keep refining the audience data available, Nielsen has evolved from diary-based data to electronic data to software at the set-top box level that allows operators to monitor channels choices and changes. In audio-based media, Arbitron's Portable People Meter recognizes today's mobile world and begins to address cross-platform measurement. It is also interesting to reflect on the U.S. Congressional involvement in television audience ratings accuracy (or lack thereof as it were) that led to the formation of what is now known as the "Media Rating Council" in the early 1960s. The time has come for social media audience research to greatly increase in sophistication, accuracy, and relevance.

When we think about social media audience size measures today, the emphasis is on opportunities to see (OTS), although almost never by this name. We might call them Impressions or Reach, but what we really mean is how many people had the potential to see this content item. There are two overarching issues here:

1. OTS is not the same as actually seeing.
2. The metrics count all possible members of the audience, regardless of whether or not they are part of the targeted audience or can even buy the product or service.

OTS is also a prevalent metric in the public relations industry, which has always focused on stating the highest possible audience measures. In traditional media, we know the probability of any one person in the audience actually seeing the article in question is a fraction of the total audience—a reasonable estimate is 10 percent or less. So OTS greatly overstates the actual number of people who saw a given article. To compound the audience overstatement, we have the practice of using audience multipliers to "credit" earned media for either a perceived credibility advantage over advertising or to account for pass-along circulation. Thankfully the practice of applying multipliers (and its evil cousin advertising value equivalency [AVEs]) is out of favor and rapidly on a path toward extinction (Michaelson and Stacks 2007; Weiner and Bartholomew 2006).

In social media one can make the case that the audience metrics situation is actually exacerbated in that the probability of any one follower seeing any one tweet, for example, is most likely an order of magnitude less than in earned media—my guesstimate is 1 percent or less. Before you dismiss this guesstimate, play around with a few Twitter factoids—the recent Pew Research study suggesting only 8 percent of Twitter users use it daily, the perishable nature of most individual's twitter streams, and the fact that a reasonably high percentage of Followers of a brand are bots, and the reality is that only a small fraction of Twitter followers actually see tweets, let alone find it interesting enough to share or comment on. And, of course, not all Facebook Likes see every post you make either. Riffing on the old, "if a tree falls in the forest …," if you tweet into the twitterverse and no one sees it does it make an impact?

Evolving from "Opportunities to See" to "Relevant Audience" Measures

Most social media campaigns have a specific target audience in mind, often described with demographics (females of ages 18 to 34), psychographics (who worry about feeding their family healthy food on a budget), and behavioral (access deal and coupon sites regularly) dimensions. Yet when it comes to reporting and measurement we take credit for the entire audience (total OTS) rather than the percentage of the audience that meets our targeting criteria. Trying to promote lingerie to 22- to 29-year-old ladies? No worries, count all your Twitter Followers and all the visitors to your website—the men, the young, and the old—everybody counts. Trying to sell camo clothing to male hunters? No worries, everybody counts—male, female, hunters, nonhunters, and People for the Ethical Treatment of Animals (PETA) members, too. Of course this all seems a little silly and strange and I suppose it would be if it wasn't the way most social audience reporting is done today. It is unusual to see someone in social media, or public relations for that matter, report only the relevant audience OTS. Why is this? I believe there are three primary reasons:

1. *Legacy*—the public relations industry has historically reported gross potential audience size rather than the relevant audience size. When

social media came around, this same orientation toward gross audience measurement was used.

2. *Data*—there is a lack of consistent social media demographic and psychographic audience data available and it often resides in channel silos rather than cross-platforms. And often the audience data from one platform (e.g., ComScore) does not match the data available from another platform (e.g., Compete).

3. *Standards*—there are no standards for social media audience metrics and no codified best practices for audience measurement.

Where Do We Go from Here?

First, we need a change in mindset of how we think about audiences. From "how many people theoretically had the potential to see our content" to "how many of the people we were targeting actually saw our content." Big audience numbers are irrelevant. Relevant audience numbers are big.

Next, as the demand for audience data that contains demographic, psychographic, and behavioral data grows, it is reasonable to assume that one or more of the large media data companies might start to aggregate and make the data available. Privacy concerns, cookies, and other issues are also in play here.

And, last but not least, industry standards for social media audience and engagement metrics and definitions are necessary for transparency and replicability that will increase credibility of social media measurement and reporting. The year 2012 will go down as the year that serious cross-industry progress on social media metrics standards began and gained momentum. There has already been a lot of progress (see the blog post "Who Are the Measurati that Are Setting Social Media Measurement Standards?" from Katie Paine 2012), and this week in Dublin, at the 4th AMEC European Summit on Measurement, the theme is around attempting to define standards for social media metrics and measurement. To tune into the debate as it occurs in Dublin, monitor #SMMStandards and #AMEC2012.

What are your thoughts on the need for social media metrics standards and the use of target rather than gross audience size estimates?

Where Is Your Organization on the Social Media Listening Maturity Model?

(July 23, 2012)

Quite often I am asked to consult with a company on their social media listening strategy. Their initial question, more times than not, is about the listening platform they should use. But it is increasingly common for the questions to be more sophisticated and the ambition behind them to be much greater. Companies with experience in social listening know that it is all too easy to focus on rudimentary analysis of brand mentions and topics, Followers, and Likes and never get to the truly actionable insights that lead to marketing or business actions. Experience in listening is an important element here but you also need a path to follow. I thought a maturity model approach to social media listening could provide a possible path to consider and would provide a construct that could be used in consulting with a company on their social listening strategy.

Maturity models are sort of hot—there seems to be a proliferation in the last two years or so. One that I find particularly insightful and helpful when thinking about social listening is Forrester's social maturity model (Corcoran 2011). Two really important points the folks at Forrester make is that listening is not the goal, social intelligence is, and that social intelligence informs actions taken by marketing or some other area of the business, *action* being the operative word here. Social intelligence is a closely related topic to social business, and if social business is more your thing, the Dachis Group has an interesting social business maturity model. Is big data more your bag? Check out IBM's big data governance model (Soares 2012). After looking at the models out there, I could not find one specific enough to social media listening so I took a stab at creating one, as shown in Figure 5.2.

There are five stages in the social media listening maturity model, beginning with reactive alerts and ending with social intelligence. Let's take a brief look at each stage and some of the overarching differences or changes one sees with social listening maturity.

Reactive alerts—Many companies or brands begin by establishing a reactive alert system that notifies them whenever their brand is mentioned or is mentioned with specific keywords. Think Google Alerts. Companies

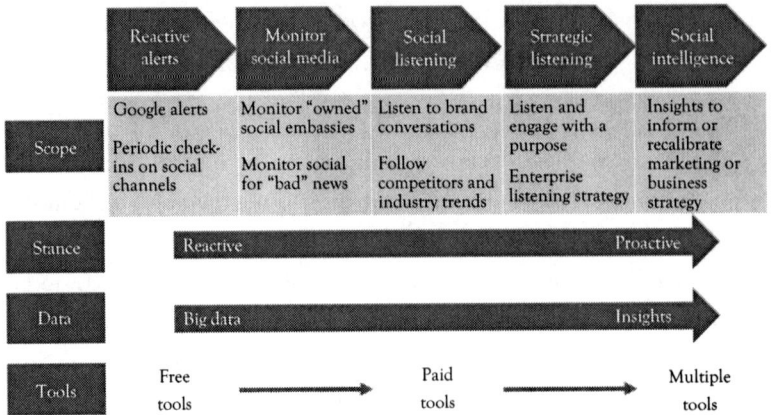

Figure 5.2 Social media listening maturity model

in this stage may only periodically check social media channels to see what may have changed or is new since the last check-in.

Monitoring social media—At the next stage, the company has begun active monitoring of all "owned" social embassies. They also are monitoring social media conversations, often focused on trying to detect any "bad" news, mentions, or conversations.

Companies in these first two stages generally have a reactive stance toward social media, viewing it as another way to find out about news and circumstances that may harm or otherwise impact the organization. It is common for companies in these stages to use one or more of the various free tools available to gather web and social media data.

Social listening—The third stage is most likely where the largest percentage of companies reside today. Companies in stage three are listening to social conversations about their company, brands, and products. They are tracking mentions of competitors and calculating share of conversation. Many also track issues and topics that are important to their brands/products/company. At this stage many begin to put additional emphasis on "who" is talking (source) not just "what" is being said (post). Most companies in the social listening phase have transitioned from free tools to paid platforms.

Companies in the first three stages often suffer from having too much data and not enough insights. They are up to their necks in "big data" but lack the experience and expertise to analyze the data and reduce it down to crisp, actionable insights supported by the data. They look for the Insight button on the tools they use but increasingly realize that insights are the product of human analysts, not tools or data.

Strategic listening—The transition to strategic listening brings with it a bias toward "listening with a purpose." I first heard this turn of phrase from my friends at Radian6 and use it often. Listening with a purpose is just that—listening to specific sets of conversations with a specific goal or objective in mind. Often in insight work, the goal or objective may take the form of a hypothesis we are trying to test. Here are a few examples of listening with a purpose:

- Listening for conversations of consumers in a particular phase of the buying decision process
- Listening to customers whose subscriptions or policies are about to expire that are expressing thoughts of changing vendors
- Identifying, tracking, and building relationships with key influencers
- Listening for consumer reactions to new packaging or product features
- Mining the emotional content of specific stakeholder groups to determine potential risk around a sensitive issue

During this phase, an enterprise listening strategy is often developed and implemented. Some also begin to integrate data from sources beyond social media—search, web analytics, and customer data for example.

Social intelligence—Forrester defines social intelligence as the process of turning social media data into actionable marketing and business strategy. Social intelligence, therefore, is not about the best times to tweet or whether or not a Twitter party would be an effective tactic; it is about informing strategic decisions that impact the company's success. For me, three concepts are crucial:

1. *Action*—Social intelligence is designed to drive true actions.
2. *Integration*—Although the definition focuses on social media data and insights, the fact is that true insights often require more than just

social data. Integrating data from multiple data sources—consumer survey, behavioral tracking, social posts, search analytics, advertising data, customer records, scan/sales data—allows for greater understanding and richer insights. Integration of multiple data types often requires multiple tools and platforms to aggregate and analyze the data.

3. *Sharing*—For social intelligence to truly take root within an organization, the data and insights should involve cross-disciplinary groups that can look at the data from different perspectives and collectively arrive at better insights than any one group could in a vacuum. The insights then need to be systematically shared broadly across the organization, so they may be acted upon in a manner that will create the most impact. Social intelligence can be a catalyst to the silos within an organization tumbling down.

Since the social listening and social intelligence "markets" are relatively immature, this model will continue to evolve and be refined.

Where is your company today on the social media listening maturity model?

Three Keys to Insight Discovery in Social Listening

(December 13, 2012)
True social insights, as opposed to social findings or social observations, have the potential to inform, shape, or drive marketing and even business strategy decisions, not just social strategy decisions. Discovering that tweeting with a link on Tuesday between 10:00 and 11:00 a.m. drives higher levels of engagement is a social *finding*, not an insight.

Social media is a microcosm of the larger big data problem/opportunity—too much data, not enough insights. Or if you prefer, too much noise, not enough signal. If you want to improve your ability to discover insights, here are three simple approaches you can take to improve your insight hunting.

First, start all analysis with a hypothesis or series of questions the analysis is designed to answer. It is much easier to prove or disprove a hypothesis, or answer specific questions, than it is to "find out what people are saying about us in social media." The more specific the request, the better the answer is going to be. The hypothesis may be one you develop based on preliminary analysis or it may come from the "customer" for the insight. Here are two examples of hypothesis:

> Conversation about us in social media is quite negative. My boss believes "everyone" is aligned against us. I disagree. My hypothesis is that there is a very vocal and active minority of consumers who are posting large volumes of negative content about us. And I believe this group is a small fraction of the total number of people who post. The majority of consumers are actually neutral toward us.
>
> When we look at Twitter, Facebook, and Blogs we see pretty low levels of conversation about our product and the medical condition it treats. We believe there is actually a fair amount of conversation, but the conversations are occurring in Forums which may not be crawled by most social listening tools.

Second, while the hypothesis is a great way to begin to focus on what is important in the data, a further focusing mechanism is the second insight discovery key—the concept of *targeted listening*. With targeted listening we are not trying to capture all conversations that mention the brand or product. That is a "boil the ocean" approach. Instead, we listen for very specific types of conversations or conversations by very specific groups of individuals within social conversations. The trick is to have the discipline to only listen to your focus areas and not be tempted to boil the ocean in hopes of finding a few pearls. Here are three examples of targeted listening strategies:

- An insurance company resists the temptation to try to capture "all" mentions of the brand and decides to focus only on conversations where customers are thinking about nonrenewal or switching companies.
- A gaming company launches a new product and listens to understand what features are being discussed, what people like most/least about the new game, and to gauge their specific reactions to the cover art.

- A consumer products company listens only to consumers who are actively involved in the purchasing process for the type of products they offer.

The third key to discovering insights is to provide context for decision-making. Remember with insights that we are trying to inform, shape, and guide decision-making. Context is incredibly important to making better decisions faster. Good social analysts understand how marketing and business work and how strategic alternatives might impact results. Understanding this helps you put your insights in the proper context for decision-making.

Here is an example of how context can lead to better decisions. Company X has a crisis. You are asked to do real-time listening of the crisis and help the public relations team decide when and how to engage in the conversation. You come back the next day with a line chart showing a large spike in content mentioning the crisis—thousands of mentions (see Figure 5.3). You know the sentiment in negative to neutral and on which channels the content appears. Unfortunately, you have not given the people deciding whether or not to engage enough information to make a decision.

What information would provide the necessary context for decision-making? What questions do we need to try to answer? Here are a few:

- How much above "normal levels" is the spike in content? (*Normative data*).

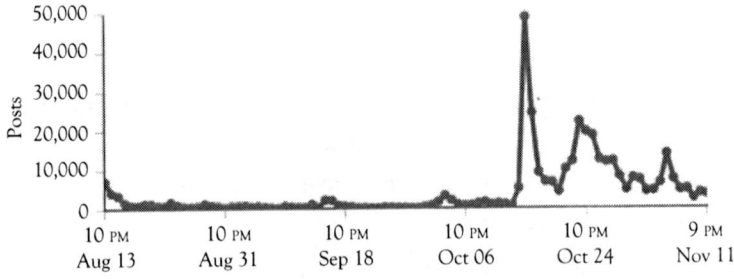

Figure 5.3 Fever graph of posts

Note: Used with Permission of Ketchum.

- How does this event compare to that event we had last year? Or, how does the event compare to competitor X who had their own crisis last year? (*Comparative data*). Comparisons help decision-makers determine "how bad is bad."
- How long do we anticipate seeing negative content at relatively high levels? (*Comparative data*). This might be the most important question to answer to provide context and guidance for the engagement decision. If we anticipate that volume will drop back to normal in a reasonable period of time, then not engaging may be a viable and effective strategy depending on the brand involved and the nature of the crisis.
- Which stakeholder groups are active in the conversations? With robust social analysis we always want to look at both the post—what is being said, and the source—who is saying it. In a crisis, who is talking is particularly important.

Normative data, comparative data, and examining both post and source data are all effective techniques to provide context for decision-making.

The tough part about discovering insights is that there are no short-cuts and it is a human activity. No social media analysis platform that I have found has an insight button. The key barrier is lack of people who understand how to search for and discover insights. I hope that these tips will make you a more effective explorer.

Social Media Measurement at a Crossroads

(August 21, 2013)

We are at a crossroads in social media measurement. Expectations for rigorous and relevant measurement have risen more quickly than delivery. Too many are fixated on quantitative outputs—speeds and feeds—at the expense of understanding the outcomes achieved by social media marketing and social business. There is still too much emphasis on vanity metrics and not enough on business results. And, if you take a step back, there is simply too much talk about all this and not enough action. At the risk of exacerbating the last point, let me explain.

Social Media Measurement Started With the Wrong Orientation

In the late 1990s and early 2000s, digital measurement focused on website analytics. The orientation was heavily quantitative. How many unique visitors? How many page views? How long did people remain on site? By 2007, with Facebook now three years old and Twitter completing its inaugural year, social media measurement was becoming a hot topic.

Early social media measurement professionals generally came from the web analytics world. Early social media measurement efforts focused on quantifying outputs and not addressing the outcome of the program. The orientation was on "How Many?" and not "What Happened?" (see Figure 5.4). The quantitative orientation also came at the expense of qualitative assessment. The emphasis was on getting easily accessible statistics and not on content analysis to understand meaning and implications. These issues remain today, although we have made significant progress toward shifting the orientation to outcomes and business results.

In the early adopter phase of social media, social media measurement was under little pressure to go beyond quantitative output analysis. Many brands, companies, and organizations viewed social media participation as a bit of an experiment to see how well it could be used within their organizations. But this was soon to change.

Figure 5.4 How or what?

Struggle Between Easy/Superficial and Hard/Meaningful

It is difficult to pinpoint when social media crossed the chasm into a mainstream business activity (see Figure 5.5). An International Data Corporation (IDC) study in the fall of 2009 suggested that the state of social media still best fit the early adopter and not mainstream use pattern at that point in time (Moran 2009). The year 2011 felt like the year the leap happened to me. With it came a new and emerging set of expectations around social media measurement.

In measurement, it is a truism that the metrics that are easiest to measure are seldom the ones that are most meaningful. It may be easy to measure outputs, but it is often much more difficult and expensive to measure outcomes. It is much easier to determine brand mentions in social media than it is to assess whether or not social programming has changed opinions and attitudes of the target. It is infinitely easier to measure unique visitors per month than it is to determine the return on investment of a social media initiative.

Now that social media is clearly a mainstream business activity, the pressure to demonstrate the impact and value of social media has greatly increased. As the resources and investment against social media and social business become meaningful line items in the budget, the game changes. Demonstrating business impact and value requires an understanding of the business model of the company or organization and how social media/business creates impact (e.g., change in awareness, increase in

Figure 5.5 Vanity measurement or business impact?

purchase consideration, and increase in active advocates around an issue) in that environment. Measuring impact is more difficult than measuring audience or engagement. It often involves primary audience research, so the price tag is higher.

This is a key struggle we face—will we continue to take the easy, less expensive, minimal-value-of-the-findings approach or we will take social media measurement to another level, focusing on outcomes, investing in audience research, and applying rigorous analytics to get at meaning and insight? The imperative is clear; how we respond will be telling.

A Final Turn to the Right

One of the key themes at this year's AMEC measurement conference in Madrid was creating a bias toward action (AMEC 2013b). The time to (just) talk about measurement is in the past; the time for action is now. I might suggest this goes double for social media measurement. Here are three areas we can address that will help make the leap from talk to action (see Figure 5.6).

- *Every social media initiative has a measurement plan.* Let's make this happen. Literally any social media initiative, program, or activity should have a measurement plan defined before implementation begins. Start with writing social media objectives that are *measurable. Align* social media metrics with

Figure 5.6 Making the move from talk to action

business KPIs. Select metrics across *multiple dimensions*—programmatic, channel-specific, and business-level metrics, for example. Or perhaps paid, owned, earned, and shared metrics if your program is integrated across these dimensions. *Collect* data. *Assess* performance against objectives. Rinse and repeat.

- *Take a stand on standards.* An exciting cross-industry effort has produced a set of proposed standards for social media metrics. Adopting standard definitions and metrics for social media is an important stage of measurement maturity that other marketing disciplines such as advertising and direct marketing have already reached.

- *Understand, articulate, and demonstrate business impact.* The heat is on to demonstrate how social media is helping drive the business or organization forward. We must do a better job of connecting the dots between business KPIs, social media objectives and social media metrics, and measurement. In some cases, we want to go beyond understanding attitudinal and behavioral changes to understand the financial value of the impact created. Capturing the financial value of social media requires expertise, data, time, and money. We would always like to measure impact, and when it makes sense, we may push further to attribute financial value.

It will be interesting to see what the next year in social media measurement brings. The move toward standardization alone should be fascinating to watch. I have tried to make the argument we are at a crossroads or inflection point in social media measurement maturity. What "worked" for us in the past will not work in the future. We know the expectations. The great unknown is how we respond.

Let's Play 20 Questions: Social Media Measurement Style

(October 1, 2013)
On August 6, I gave a webinar for Carma, co-sponsored by *PRNews*, called "Social Media Measurement at a Crossroads." The webinar focused

on the current state of social media measurement with an emphasis on efforts to develop social media metrics standards. There were many good questions asked by the webinar participants. I thought it might be fun to capture 20 of the questions and share the answers I gave in response. And it might be cool if you disagree with an answer, to share your different opinion in the comments.

Q1. What level of social media measurement do you think should be taught at undergraduate level in public relations or communications degree courses?

Most schools only require one research class in undergraduate education. In this class, all forms of research including measurement are covered. I think all schools should have one general research and analytics course and another specifically for measurement. I would cover traditional and digital in both courses with an emphasis on digital techniques.

Q2. What needs to happen for businesses to be able to integrate Communications Performance Management with Business Performance Management?

Did Philip Sheldrake ask you to ask this question? Well, the first thing that would have to happen is for companies to start demanding it. I've not seen much demand for this. Once demand builds, smart people will figure out how to make it happen. The AMEC Social Media Measurement Committee is going to take on the challenge of developing a balanced scorecard approach to the social media valid framework to see where that takes us.

Q3. Speaking about social business, are you suggesting that social media become the strategic imperative with marketing, customer service, public relations, employee engagement subordinate? So these functions will be driven by social media specialists?

No, not at all. I think what we'll see if that social media permeates all of these functions and creates new capabilities and connections between groups and between customers and companies. It is up to public relations or human resource people to learn something about social media. Social media specialists are not going to take over the world.

Q4. Are the proposed standard social media metrics valid for native ads as well?

I have not thought much about this, but my initial reaction is that the metrics for native ads would be same. A promoted tweet would have the same engagement metrics as any other tweet, although one would certainly hope the performance on some of the metrics would be better.

Q5. What do you mean when you say triage social media content for customer service and support?

This would refer to evaluating and routing social content to different entities or people within an organization (customer care vs. technical support vs. legal, for example) that are best able to understand and act on the feedback and/or respond to the post.

Q6. Don, what do you put more emphasis on these days, Likes and Follows or Shares and Comments?

I believe that the emphasis should be on the stronger indications of engagement, shares, and comments, than on simple Likes and Follows.

Q7. How well-known and widely accepted are the Conclave standards in the social space as a whole?

The first complete set of standards were published in early June 2013. They are known by social media measurement insiders, but I think it is fair to say that they are not yet widely known. We need to promote their existence and use.

Q8. How would you measure perception and attitudes through social media?

Generally, we would measure consumer conversations about a topic and then do some analysis to see if there are clusters of comments that represent different and distinct viewpoints, attitudes, or opinions about the issue or topic. We might also want to do an audience segmentation analysis to see how these attitudes differ by stakeholder group.

Q9. Any specific comments geared toward nonprofit organizations?

The basics of measurement—write measurable goals, align goals with organizational KPIs, assess performance against targets—are the same for for-profit and not-for-profit organizations. How value is created is the primary difference.

Q10. Any suggestions to measure business impact for B2B organizations? Is there a way to understand the impact of social media for B2B organizations?

Most B2B companies have a focus on sales leads. Therefore, demonstrating how social media are helping create leads or improve lead closure rates is important. There are a lot of uses of social listening in B2B companies as well—how the company is positioned on key issues, who is talking about the company, how products and services are being discussed, and so forth.

Q11. What are your favorite tools to use in terms of actually measuring your programs/channels/campaigns? Do you identify the tools as you are defining the metrics (do we have the ability to measure X, Y, Z?) or do you select tools after you define your metrics (this is what we need to know, let's find A, B, C solutions to measure these things)?

Generally, Google Analytics, a social listening platform (Radian6, Brandwatch, Netbase, Visible, and so forth), channel analytics programs such as Facebook Insights, and also Excel. Ideally you should define metrics first, then the data required for each metric, then look at the tools best able to get the specific data you need.

Q12. What are the most common or most surprising questions you have gotten from chief marketing officers (CMOs) or other key stakeholders regarding social media measurement?

CMOs want to know how social media contributes value to marketing—if they are sales-funnel-oriented they want to know how social media are helping drive the funnel, for example. They are also interested if you are helping on front-end or downstream funnel metrics.

Q13. What advice do you have for small businesses for use of and measuring success of social media campaigns effectively (few resources)?

Start with the free tools (Hootsuite, Excel, Facebook Insights, Twitter Analytics, Google Analytics) and then work your way up to some of the paid social listening platforms. There is no "best" platform to start with—it really depends on your needs and what you intend to do with the platform. Many companies start with measuring their own channels and evolve to listening to earned/ shared social conversations.

Q14. Which social media analytics do the C-suite find most valuable?
The C-suite doesn't really care about social media analytics so much; they care about how social media is helping drive the business metrics forward. That said, C-level folks are usually interested in competitive benchmarking in social media and positioning on key issues and topics that are important to the business. Anything pertaining to online reputation is also an area of interest for many.

Q15. How do you determine what are the correct things to measure?
Measure what matters to the organization. Measurement is about performance against objectives, so make sure your measurement program is aligned with business objectives. Don't measure "social media," measure what you are trying to accomplish with social media.

Q16. How can someone who is interested in the movement toward standard metrics get involved in helping to move the public relations industry forward? In other words, how can someone get involved in the debate?
I would suggest interacting directly on the www.smmstandards.org website. Volunteer to help. Leave suggestions. You could also get involved through one of the public relations associations—IPR, PRSA, or IPRA (International Public Relations Association).

Q17. What software would you recommend be used by public relations firms to most cost effectively measure social media efforts for clients?
A good social listening platform, Google Analytics, Facebook Insights, and the other packages offered by the channels, and good old Excel. Beyond that it really depends on the nature of the social media effort.

Q18. I think a lot of the issue with measurement is confidence in the measurer (i.e., your source). Whenever you cross-reference measurements (e.g., what Google analytics says vs. what your web marketing automation says, such as HubSpot), you can get wildly different answers. That has stopped me from putting too much faith in my metrics process. Thoughts?
I might separate the issue of the measurer from the sources of data—really two different issues. Regarding sources of data, this is a true issue in that different databases yield different estimates for things

such as audience size. Compete versus ComScore is a notorious example. However, I don't think this is a reason to not measure. It simply means that we must state assumptions and sources and be consistent over time in using comparable sources. I believe that standard metrics will eventually lead to sanctioned sources for audience data such as Arbitron (now Nielsen Audio) for radio or Nielsen for TV.

Q19. Let's say that a social media post leads someone to a landing page, but they do not take immediate action. But they come back the next week and complete the conversion funnel. How do you credit the original social media post ... is this a matter of tracking cookies for x number of days? What is practical?

Yep, most people count the first click and then track for a period of time depending on the type of product. It gets even more complicated if you try to suggest that credit should also be given to what happened before the first social media click—for example, money invested in building the brand. Value attribution is an inexact science for sure, with lots of assumptions and compromises.

Q20. What are best ways to measure target audience reach and engagement rather than wide general reach?

Thanks for asking this. The best way to measure is to clearly define your target. If the target is females of ages 18 to 34, then you should only take credit for reach and engagement of this specific audience only. Given that most tools rely on voluntary bio data, the information is inconsistent and difficult to come by.

CHAPTER 6

The Deadly Sins of Advertising Value Equivalents

I'll never forget the first time I met Don; he blasted me over lunch about AVE and I still have scars on my rear end! But we ended up good friends—of course, I gave up AVE, too.
—Angela Jeffrey, Vice President Brand Manager at Advertising Benchmark Index

This chapter includes:

- The dangerous notion of advertising value equivalents (AVEs)
- The harm AVEs have brought to the public relations profession
- Top reasons for AVEs to be abandoned in public relations measurement

AVEs (Advertising Value Equivalents) Revisited

(December 24, 2007)

Generally speaking, advertising delivers a lower return on investment (ROI) than public relations. So why do we want to compare our results to those of an ad? Because it is a path of least resistance to calculating ROI, flawed as it is. Many people obviously believe that a poor metric for ROI is better than none at all.

So, in the spirit of the 12 Days of Christmas, here are the 12 reasons why AVEs are a poor metric for public relations. And one rationale for using them that makes at least a little sense.

1. Advertisements and editorial articles are perceived differently by receivers/readers. Editorial material benefits from the credibility of a third-party (the publication) by earning, not paying, its way into the magazine, newspaper, or broadcast.

2. AVEs equate an article with the appearance cost of an advertisement. It does not speak at all to the results or impact that the article may have on a reader. Advertisers do not judge the success of advertising on how much the insertions cost. The true value of an ad or article is in what it does—the outcome or impact, not the cost of appearance.

3. AVEs do not address the value of several important aspects of public relations including strategic counsel, crisis communications, grass-roots, viral campaigns, or public affairs. In other words, AVEs reduce public relations to just the media dimension by only assigning a value in this area. If only AVEs are used to assess public relations value, the results will be much understated when considering the totality of value delivered by public relations.

4. AVEs cannot measure the value of keeping a client with potentially negative news (e.g., layoff, scandal) out of the media, yet that may be the primary objective of the public relations professional. How much is it worth for a troubled company to not appear in the *Wall Street Journal*? AVEs cannot address this.

5. Impression information for public relations is somewhat inconsistent. Online impressions figures are not as reliable as print or broadcast, and are generally believed to be overstated. The fact that they are inflated skews AVE calculations to (pick one: somewhat, very, grossly) overstate the value of online media, often assigning unbelievable values to online articles compared to their print counterparts. This hurts credibility and believability.

6. AVEs do not properly distinguish between hits/articles that appear in "high value" columns or publications and articles in more general or generic publications. The calculation is based on ad cost only. The value of appearing in a Walt Mossberg column in the *Wall Street Journal* or on *Oprah* with your new book far exceeds the cost of an advertisement in the *Wall Street Journal* or on *Oprah* due to the implied or explicit endorsement with earned media. Just look at what Oprah's endorsement has done for Obama recently.

7. Advertising and public relations actually work together synergistically, yet AVEs treat them essentially as equals or alternatives. Ads that run in a climate of positive publicity actually receive lift from the public relations. Conversely, ads run in an environment of negative publicity will likely not be successful and/or may be perceived negatively by consumers/customers.

8. AVEs are generally calculated by mainly, or only, taking into account the physical size of the article, and then equating that to the cost/value of an advertisement of the same size. Often, *article valence* is not even considered, so a predominantly negative article would add positively to the overall AVE calculation. Others count the size of the entire article, even if only one paragraph directly addresses the company in question.

9. Some groups have devised their own ways to calculate AVEs. Public relations articles are generally rated or scored as part of an algorithm used to calculate AVEs. Factors considered might include brand prominence within the article, competitive mentions, overall article tonality, and, finally, size/length of the article. The problem here is that there is no standard way to "score" public relations articles to implement an AVE system.

10. If you get a hit on the front page of a newspaper or a cover story in a magazine, there is no way to calculate an advertising equivalency since advertising space is never sold in these locations.

11. AVE results can be misleading. AVEs may be trending up while important metrics such as message communication, share of favorable positioning, and share of positive press are falling. Objects may appear larger than they really are.

12. AVEs only apply to traditional media. What is the AVE of a positive conversation about your company on a leading blog?

If you are still searching for a rationale for using AVEs, there is one that has some merit in my opinion. That is the economic argument that advertising rates are established in a free market system. Publishers can only charge what advertisers are willing to pay for a page in their publication. Essentially the value of that page is established by this free market system. Of course what appears on this page is not considered in the value determination. I would suggest that one refer to the value of a page determined in this way as the "Media Value" rather than the Advertising Value. By using the term Media Value, one eliminates the uncomfortable and unjustified comparison of an article generated by public relations with an advertisement. You are merely suggesting that the page has a value and you use that value to determine how much the public relations content is therefore "worth." Media Value is still not a great way to assess the value generated by public relations for many of the reasons stated previously, but it seems to me to be less objectionable than AVEs.

What Is That Hit in the (Insert Major Publication Name Here) Worth? Nothing, Unless It Creates Engagement

(May 7, 2009)

A few months back someone posed a question in a LinkedIn discussion group wondering how much the major hit in *USA Today* he had just got for a client was worth. Obviously he is not the first public relations professional to ask this question. Before pondering the answer, there are several questions we should address first:

> How many people in our target audience had an opportunity to see the placement?
> How many actually saw it?
> Of these, how many actually read the article?
> Of those reading it, did it change their thinking in any way?
> Did they forward it on to others?
> Mention it in a phone conversation with a friend?
> Visit a website?
> Digg it.
> Tweet it?
> Blog about it?
> Buy it?...

While one must have Exposure before Engagement, much like Awareness must precede Purchase Consideration, true value creation begins at the Engagement stage. Using old school language, value occurs with

Outcomes, not Outputs. Seems simple enough, yet the majority of public relations professionals are still relying on output-oriented metrics such as clip counts and AVEs to judge success. Public relations pros who are savvy about social media seem to be further evolved. They understand that true value is not in the content (an output) per se, but in the level of engagement caused by the content.

Are you looking for value in all the right or wrong places?

AVEs Are a Disease—Here's a Little Vaccine

(April 16, 2011)
One of the truly insidious aspects of public relations measurement is the use of advertising value equivalency (AVEs) or media value to assign financial value to public relations outputs. It is a highly flawed, path-of-least-resistance attempt to calculate Return on Investment (ROI) for public relations. To make matters worse, the practice has clearly moved into social media measurement as well. For example, research studies that attempt to monetize the value of a Facebook Fan/Liker by attributing a cost per mille (CPM) value from the advertising world. Online media impact rankings also utilize equivalent paid advertising costs to assign monetary value to online news and social media. AVE is like a disease that has infected and spread throughout the public relations industry.

In June 2010, the public relations industry came together in Barcelona to draft the *Barcelona Principles*[1] (Institute for Public Relations 2010), a set of seven principles of good measurement intended to provide guideposts for the industry. The principle that has generated the most conversation is this one.

AVE Is Not the Value of Public Relations

While many of the *Measurati* have been preaching against AVEs for years, there now appears to be a critical mass of outrage that may kill the practice

---

[1] The *Barcelona Principles* was updated to the Barcelona Principles 2.0 in September 2015 (Institute for Public Relations 2015). For more information, please visit www.instituteforpr.org/barcelona-principles-2-0-updated-2015/

in the coming years. Here are four compelling reasons why I believe we must make this happen—the sooner the better.

AVES Do Not Measure Outcomes

AVEs equate an article with the appearance cost of an advertisement. It does not speak at all to the results or impact that the article may have on a reader. Advertisers do not judge the success of advertising on how much the insertions cost. Imagine an advertising manager being asked by his or her boss, "How are we doing in advertising this year?," and them replying, "Great! We have spent $500,000 so far!" The true value of public relations or social media is not the appearance cost, but what happened as a *result* of the public relations or social media effort—the impact it has on brand, reputation, and marketing. You will note that the Barcelona Principles also call for a focus on measuring outcomes and not (just) outputs. What happened as a result of media coverage is inherently more interesting and valuable than how much coverage was obtained.

AVEs Reduce Public Relations to Media Relations

You are, or become, what you measure. AVEs do not address the impact or value of several important aspects of public relations including strategic counsel, crisis communications, grassroots efforts, viral campaigns, or public affairs. In other words, AVEs reduce public relations to just the media dimension by only assigning a value in this area. If only AVEs are used to assess public relations value, the results will understate the totality of value delivered by public relations. AVEs also cannot measure the value of keeping a client with potentially negative news out of the media, yet that may be the primary objective of the public relations practitioner.

AVEs Fly in the Face of Integrated Measurement

Good marketing, branding, and reputation campaigns have always been integrated to varying degrees. The digitization of our lives has accelerated integration.

Advertising and public relations actually work together synergistically, yet AVEs treat them as cost alternatives. Studies have shown ads that run in a climate of positive publicity actually receive lift from the public relations. Conversely, ads run in an environment of negative publicity will likely not be successful and/or may be perceived negatively by consumers. We have seen exposure to brand advertising increases conversion rates in social channels. Integrated campaigns and programs require integrated measurement. AVEs don't play well in this world. They are analog and segregated in a digital and integrated world.

AVEs Provide No Diagnostic Value

Too much measurement energy is focused on score-keeping and not diagnostics. This is one reason why single-number metrics such as the Klout score and others have great appeal to many. However, measurement is fundamentally about assessing performance against objectives with sufficient detail and granularity to determine what is working and what is not. AVEs fail miserably in this regard. AVE results can actually be misleading and result in false positives. AVEs may be trending up while important metrics such as message communication, share of favorable positioning, and share of voice are falling. Unfortunately, AVEs provide neither a valid single-number score nor any diagnostic value.

Some have said that the *Barcelona Principles* are the "end of AVEs." I would agree directionally with that statement with one minor addition, Barcelona was the "beginning of the end of AVEs." Awareness of the practice and recognition of its flaws are at an all-time high in our industry. More education and evangelism are required. Understanding concepts such as impact, tangible value, intangible value, and (true) ROI helps foster much more sophisticated conversation about the total value delivered by public relations and social media. AVEs are a disease; education and knowledge are the vaccine. AVEs won't die easily. The momentum generated by the Barcelona event has provided focus and intent. It is up to all of us to make AVEs a thing of the past.

AVEs Don't Describe the Value of Media Coverage, They Sensationalize It

(June 26, 2011)
Saturday, *Wall Street Journal* (WSJ) columnist Carl Bialik, The Numbers Guy, addressed the subject of advertising value equivalency (AVE) (Bialik

2011). This is perhaps the first example of a mainstream media publication shining a light on the controversial practice of AVEs.

The primary reason that AVEs exist is because they are perceived to be a way to attribute value to programs that would otherwise be difficult to value directly. They are a path of least resistance approach to ROI calculations, but not a valid one. Let's take a deeper dive into the three specific examples in the WSJ story, ask the tough questions, and discuss more valid ways to think about value attribution and ROI.

American Airlines

You can enjoy both questionable valuation techniques and hyperbole in this article. American Airlines stands to "make boatloads of cash" and "the airline company could gain as much as $95.9 million of exposure." Of really, let's take a closer look.

The most incredible part of this financial calculation is the financial calculation itself. The calculation is apparently based on sign placement within the arena and presumably the "impressions" the brand will receive when people attending the venue see the signage and when TV cameras catch the signs when showing the scoreboard or during the action. This is a very passive form of advertising that should have as its objective either creating top-of-mind awareness or perhaps creating more brand affinity. Rather than using an advertising equivalency model that has no validity, a true measurement of the value created by naming rights would ask a series of questions designed to determine the actual, tangible (or even intangible) impact on the business:

- *Revenue*: Can incremental revenue generation in the form of higher passenger miles be directly attributed to the exposure created by the naming rights? Is it possible that incremental revenue would actually be realized on a game by game basis, or would any positive impact be realized over a longer time horizon? Have new customers been created as a direct result of the exposure generated by the naming rights?
- *Brand*: Can the increased exposure lead to people perceiving the brand differently and can the difference translate into

higher transactional revenues generated or increased brand loyalty?

So where exactly are the "boatloads of cash" American Airlines made? Are they hitting the income statement in the form of incremental revenue or enhanced brand loyalty (repeat business)? Are they residing on the balance sheet in terms of brand goodwill? Given that American's parent company AMR lost $11.5B in the first decade of the 21st century, its last profitable year was 2007, and they are projected to lose money in 2011 and 2012, they could use the cash. Perhaps they could use it to fund a "bags fly free" program or for enhancing their Advantage program to create more brand loyalty. I would strongly suspect that American's shareholders would prefer a do-over on the investments made on naming rights to the "boatloads of cash" they are now enjoying from the investment.

Couple Won't Cash in on Kiss

Fifteen minutes of fame is rarely worth $10 million. In this case, the celebrity agent is suggesting the news value of the coverage generated by the kiss is somehow equivalent to advertising value and assigns what appears to be an arbitrary and ridiculously high value to it. (He later admits he just made the number up.) Just how was the couple going to monetize their 15 minutes of fame? Yes, they turned down a few talk show opportunities and perhaps the *National Enquirer* would have thrown a few dollars their way for an exclusive, but the assertion that any major brand would have paid them to endorse their product is wildly speculative.[2] I would guess that if you did a survey after the event, a small number of people would remember seeing the coverage, and a very small percentage of the people who did see it would have recalled Scott Jones's name. So perhaps Mr. Jones walked away from tens of thousands of potential dollars in the short term, but nowhere near the sensationalized estimate of $10 million. Fifteen minutes of fame might be worth $10,000, but certainly not $10 million.

---

[2] Editor: For more background information on this story, please visit www.scotsman.com/news/couple-won-t-cash-in-on-10-million-kiss-1-1692861

Obama Enjoys a Guinness

So Guinness is a winner and received $20 million worth of "free publicity?" What was the outcome of the publicity? Again, in order to determine the value of the "free publicity" (this term is despised in the public relations industry by the way), Guinness would have to be able to measure incremental revenues directly attributable to the publicity generated. Did sales of Guinness increase as a result? Were new customers created? Did existing customers feel compelled to drink even more? What was the value of the incremental sales? These are much more difficult questions to answer but are the correct ones to ask in order to measure the publicity. Not by focusing on the mythical value of the coverage as measured by flawed advertising equivalency, but measuring the outcome or what happened as a result of the publicity. The assertion that President Obama's image was softened and will help keep him in the public's favor is highly dubious thinking. Perhaps it helps him in Boston, but in the grand scheme of things, this is a presidential image nonevent.

Beginning of the End?

Beginning last summer in Barcelona, the public relations industry has come together to publicly state that advertising value equivalency is not a valid measure of public relations. The so-called *Barcelona Principles* are explicit against AVEs and also call for a focus on measuring outcomes and not (just) outputs. While it will take some time for the public relations industry to totally leave AVEs behind, there is a lot of momentum right now to make this happen sooner rather than later. No serious measurement effort can use advertising value equivalency to attribute value and be credible.

CHAPTER 7

Thus Spoke the *Measurati*

I have served with Don on the IPR Measurement Commission, and consider him one of the most giving souls in our field. Smart and selfless, always ready to debate ideas without ego—and share his wit and wisdom with all he encounters.

—Tim Marklein, Founder and CEO of Big Valley Marketing

This chapter includes:

- The *Barcelona Principles* and the biggest takeaways from the Second European Summit on Measurement
- How much companies spend on public relations, how the public relations organization fits within the overall organizational structure, and companies' budgeting for public relations measurement and evaluation as well as the best practices
- The heated debate over relationship measurement

Integrated Approaches to Social Media and Public Relations Measurement Will Yield More Actionable Insights

(April 21, 2009)

With more public relations programming occurring online than ever before, the measurement world seems increasingly seduced by readily available and increasingly sophisticated web analytics. Indeed, with respect to social media in particular, it seems the majority of thought leadership in measurement today is being driven by web analytics gurus and *not* measurement gurus (there are a few exceptions of course). No real problem here since web analytics add real value in understanding online behavior. They do a good job of understanding the what, the who, and the where. And the cost is often quite low to obtain the data.

A concern with a singular emphasis on web analytics is that they do not provide any real insights into *the whys driving the behavior*. What are people thinking when they interact with our content? Are we influencing the way they perceive the brand or company? What are the reasons they buy or not buy a product? These insights not only help us better measure our results, but they also help inform the development of better and more effective future programming.

I don't see this as an either/or proposition. The best answer is both. And add in content analysis too as a diagnostic tool. A holistic, integrated social media/public relations measurement approach that utilizes web analytics, content analysis, and primary audience research adds measurement richness and provides valuable formative insights. All research/measurement is good. More is better. Holistic is best.

You Might Be a Public Relations/Social Media Redneck If...

(March 23, 2009)
(With tongue firmly in cheek and apologies to Jeff Foxworthy)

Getting That Big Hit in a Daily Newspaper or National Magazine Is Your Primary Public Relations Objective

While traditional media relations will continue to play a role in public relations programming, its importance and impact is shrinking at an alarming rate with each new publishing industry announcement of shuttered operations, three-day-a-week printing schedules, and Chapter 11 filings. Over 120 newspapers have folded entirely (Chen 2009).[1] Anorexic-thin magazines appear starved for advertising. To compound the issue, according to the latest *Edelman Trust Barometer*,[2] only 44 percent of

---

[1] For more information, please visit www.cnn.com/2009/US/03/19/newspaper.decline.layoff/index.html

[2] For the most recent *Edelman Trust Barometer* report (2016), please visit http://www.edelman.com/insights/intellectual-property/2016-edelman-trust-barometer/

consumers trust what they read in magazines and 34 percent trust what they read in newspapers (Edelman 2009). Shrinking footprint, combined with shrinking credibility, does not portend well for traditional print media.

The best public relations programs today take a broad, holistic view of the various avenues to engage with customers and prospects—traditional media, social media, community involvement, grassroots events—and attempt to do so in ways the customer/prospect respects and prefers.

Your Measurement Program Key Metrics Include Number of Hits, Impressions and Ad Values/AVEs

It is fine to include a couple of volume-oriented metrics such as number of unique articles or net positive opportunities to see (OTS) in your program, but these sorts of metrics do nothing to capture the value created by your program. In order to capture value, we must understand the audience effects or outcomes of public relations programming. Emphasis on output metrics like these may also be a reflection of a program oriented toward traditional media. Traditional media metrics do not translate well to social media where the name of the game is engagement and not (just) eyeballs. Double redneck points if you are using multipliers on impressions and/or advertising value equivalents (AVEs) to assign financial value to media hits.

The Big Social Media Question You/Your Department Have Been Asked to Answer Is "Should Our CEO Start a Blog?"

The problem is that this is almost always the wrong question at the time it is asked. There are larger, more contextual, ones to ask first. When a company begins to think about using social media, a CEO blog is often the first tactic considered. The prospective blog can potentially become a solution in search of a problem.

Take a step back and put the prospective blog in context by thinking through the bigger questions first. What key concepts and terms are strategically important to the company? Can we develop a *thought leadership platform* designed to enhance relevance, credibility, and authority in key areas? Do we have anything important to add to the conversation? Who from our company should be the voice of the company in key strategic areas? Does this individual currently have authority in this area? Is a blog a good strategy/tactic to deploy?

Your Communications Program Attempts to Control More Than Contribute

While much advancement in communications theory has occurred since the Transmission and Direct Injection models of the 1950s, the mindset and behavior of many public relations practitioners seems trapped in this "message as a drug" mentality. We want to control the message, manage our relationships, and otherwise wield direct influence over our stakeholders. This command and control mindset is truly out of phase with social media/market dynamics today. What is needed is a shift away from control toward contribution. How can you contribute to the conversation? What content can you provide the community would find of value? How can we give people a reason to talk about our brand?

As an industry we must become more comfortable participating rather than orchestrating.

You Are Thinking Vertically and Tops-Down Rather Than Horizontally and Non-Hierarchical

Many comments on social media posts immediately speak to the wonders of synchronous communication—creating a dialogue rather than a monologue. While synchronous communication has great value in gathering feedback and creating some level of dialogue, it remains a form of vertical communication. In social media, however, the world is flat or horizontal. Every piece of research I have seen suggests that consumers value the opinions of other consumers, "people just like them" more than they do companies or media pundits. The greater value in social media is peer-to-peer horizontal communication, broadly referred to as WOM, or word-of-mouth. Taking a spin on the old global/local saying, the public relations profession needs to "act vertically but think horizontally ...."

The Barcelona Principles: Leaders Speak

(June 23, 2010)

Well, the Second European Summit on Measurement held last week in Barcelona has come and gone, but its impact may be felt for some time to come. The summit was organized by the International Association for the Measurement and Evaluation of Communication (AMEC) and the Institute for Public Relations. The most notable outcome of the summit was the creation of the *Barcelona Declaration of Research Principles*.[3] The *Principles* were debated and voted upon by about 200 delegates representing 33 countries and 5 global public relations and measurement organizations (AMEC, IPR, PRSA, ICCO, The Global Alliance). David Rockland, PhD chaired the debate.

Here are the *Barcelona Declaration of Research Principles*:

1. Goal setting and measurement are fundamental aspects of any public relations programs.
2. Media measurement requires quantity and quality—cuttings in themselves are not enough.
3. Advertising Value Equivalents (AVEs) do not measure the value of public relations and do not inform future activity.
4. Social media can and should be measured.
5. Measuring outcomes is preferred to measuring media results.
6. Business results can and should be measured where possible.
7. Transparency and replicability are paramount to sound measurement.

I asked three of the leaders of the conference to comment on four questions regarding the summit and what it may mean for the future of measurement. The leaders are:

- *Barry Leggetter*, FPRCA, FCIRR, Executive Director of AMEC (barryleggetter@amecorg.com).

---

[3] For a *Barcelona Principles 2.0* updated in September 2015, please visit www.instituteforpr.org/barcelona-principles-2-0-updated-2015/

- *Pauline Draper-Watts,* Chairperson of the Institute for Public
  Relations, Commission for Public Relations Measurement
  and Evaluation (pauline.s.draper@gmail.com).
- *David Rockland, PhD,* Partner/CEO, Ketchum Pleon Change
  and Managing Director, Global Research (David.Rockland@
  ketchum.com).

Here are their thoughts on the summit:

*Q1. For those not able to attend the summit, how would you briefly
describe what they missed?*

BL: A milestone moment when delegates from 33 countries agreed to
take program measurement more seriously, starting with the aban-
donment of AVEs.

DR: Missed a great opportunity to network with colleagues from
33 countries, hear some engaging speakers, and be part of a moment
in time where the industry first adopted a set of measurement
principles.

*Q2. From your perspective, what are the two or three most significant out-
comes of the Second European Summit on Measurement?*

BL: For AMEC to be successful in getting five global organizations
on the same platform for the first time and talk from the same
page about the need for the public relations and media intelligence
industry to act—not just talk—about improved methods of program measurement.

That the summit achieved its own breakthrough status in receiving
speaker support from senior level clients of global organizations
such as FedEx Corporation, Yahoo, Royal Philips Electronics,
Nissan, Telefónica, Banco Santander, and others.

PD-W: The percentages (voting) in favor for each of the *Barcelona
Principles* following the discussion.

DR: To me a significant outcome was a gathering of the industry in a
manner where ideas were shared, friendships and partnership ext-
ended, and we agreed as an industry to look ahead to how we can do
what we do better and professionalize the practice of public relations.

*Q3. How do you hope agencies, companies, and organizations operation-
alize the seven principles?*

BL: I introduced quality management processes when a director of Porter Novelli in the United Kingdom in the 1990s—the first agency in the world to make this commitment. It became part of our agency's way of working. I hope agencies, companies, and organizations will similarly make the same commitment to the *Barcelona Principles* and introduce more stretching methods of program measurement on all programs.

PD-W: Integrating them into the culture and corporate language within the organization so that they are lived out in practice.

DR: My hope would be that first the principles are widely talked about and become SOP (standard operating procedure) for what we do. Second, that the term AVE disappears along with the incredibly counter-productive debate around this subject that has distracted the industry from its own development. And third, that each organization adapts the *Principles* into their own words and practices; when we see them translated into the languages of the 33 countries represented at the Summit, we'll know it worked.

Q4. Please complete this sentence: A year from now, we will know the Second European Summit on Measurement was successful …

BL: … if when I judge my next public relations Awards schemes, public relations consultancies, and company in-house public relations teams are putting more effort into the Program Measurement heading on the award entry as they are now doing to demonstrating creativity!

PD-W: … the *Barcelona Principles* (modified to reflect the comments made at the summit and submitted afterward) are not only adopted but also put into practice throughout the industry.

DR: … if we don't hear public relations professionals continue to complain we don't have a "seat at the table" because we lack the metrics and measurement approaches other disciplines have.

Keeping it real … and transparent

- *I am a member of the Institute for Public Relations, Commission on Public Relations Measurement and Evaluation*
- *My agency, Fleishman–Hillard, is a member of AMEC*
- *Ketchum is a sister Omnicom agency.*

GAP IV Study Points Out Measurement Gap

(May 8, 2006)

Results of the fourth annual *Public Relations Generally Accepted Practices Study* (GAP IV)[4] were released today (Swerling et al. 2005). The study is published by the USC Annenberg Strategic Public Relations Center (SPRC), and is intended to provide the public relations profession with data on evaluation, organization, budgeting, emerging trends, use of outside agencies, perceptions of the public relations function, and other important topics.

The study has several interesting findings, but let's take a look at what the findings say about Evaluation/Measurement:

- Respondents spent only 4 percent of their total public relations budgets on evaluation.
- "Ability to Quantify Results" (12 percent) ranked low on the reasons a company would choose to use an outside agency ("Additional arms and legs" (51 percent) and "Complements our internal capabilities" (47 percent) were the two highest-ranked factors).
- Sixty-four percent of all respondents (77 percent of Fortune 500 respondents) report to the C-Suite in their organizations.
- The differences in metrics used by organizations where public relations reports to the C-Suite versus those used where public relations reports to Marketing are dramatic. C-Suite metrics tend to be more strategic and organizationally focused while metrics used by those reporting to Marketing were more media and sales-oriented.
- "Influence on corporate reputation" has been the highest scoring metric in each of the four GAP studies, yet as the authors point out, "there are currently no consistently reliable, generally-accepted, quantifiable methods for correlating public relations activities with reputation."
- Public relations is seen as contributing to the bottom line success of the company (5.30 vs. top-ranked finance at 5.59).

---

[4] *The author is a member of the Professional Advisory Committee for the GAP Study.*

To amplify the fourth point, in companies reporting to the C-Suite, it was significantly more likely the following metrics were used for evaluation:

1. Crisis avoidance/mitigation
2. Influence on corporate culture
3. Influence on corporate reputation.

In companies where public relations reports to Marketing, it was significantly more likely the following metrics were used:

1. Contribution to sales
2. Total circulation of clips
3. Total number of clips.

To me, there are two key learnings from the study:

- Confirming my personal experience and observations (*more information in article "Left Brain Right for the Times" in Chapter 8*), public relations increasingly is reporting to the C-Suite and is seen as playing a strategic role within organizations, and
- There is a tremendous gap between what most companies actually measure today and the new requirements to measure how public relations is impacting the organization.

The *measurement gap* refers to the fact that the measurement industry today is focused on media content analysis (outputs measurement) while organizations increasingly value public relations for our contributions in moving the needle on reputation, culture, or sales (outcomes). We may have great data on number of impressions or percent of articles containing key messages, but how are we proving the value of public relations' contribution to the more strategic outcomes the C-Suite demands? This is a great challenge to the measurement community—we are not necessarily measuring the right things (media clips), and lack agreed-upon metrics and approaches for the types of measurement our new environment demands. We need to evaluate the tangible contributions of public relations (e.g., sales) as well as the intangible (e.g., brand or reputation). And we need to not only look at public relations' contribution to sales, but to public relations' contribution in reducing costs (e.g., regulation or litigation) and reducing risks (e.g., new product introductions, downsizing). So many challenges—so little time.

Outputs or Outcomes or Both?

(May 15, 2006)

In a recent post following up on the Gap IV study, Sherrilynne of Strive public relations poses the question in the headline above when referring to determining the true value of public relations. So what is the right answer? Is it Outputs, Outcomes, or both?

Of course the right answer is *both*. As I pointed out in my post on the Gap IV study ("Gap IV Study Points Out Measurement Gap"), the majority of public relations measurement firms today concentrate on media content analysis (outputs) while companies want to know how public relations is contributing to business objectives (outcomes). Hence the "Gap." And the "Gap" may be widening as pressure increases to prove the business benefit and return on investment for public relations. While this suggests that we need more focus and resources on Outcome measurement, it does not suggest that it should be thought of as an either/or proposition.

Measurement of public relations Outputs provides valuable diagnostic information to help answer the question, "Is our public relations campaign working?" Are we receiving coverage in our target publications? How favorable is the coverage? How prominently is our brand/company being featured in the stories? How often are our key messages being included, and with what interpretation? All of this data should be analyzed, and discussed by the public relations team, with an eye toward improving public relations efforts going forward.

Too often, public relations outputs are merely used to keep score and not as a diagnostic tool. So the answer is both—outputs and outcomes are valuable—but the orientation of how we use the output data could be improved.

Fifth GAP Study Delivers Industry Benchmarking Data ... and Best Practices

(May 28, 2008)

The University of Southern California's Annenberg School for Communication has released their fifth *Public Relations/Communications Generally Accepted Practices Study* (Swerling et al. 2007). GAP is one of the most, if not the most, comprehensive studies of key issues impacting public relations practitioners. It provides data addressing such key questions as, how much companies spend on public relations and their public relations agencies; how the public relations organization fits within the overall organizational structure; and respondents' attitudes about, and budgeting for, public relations measurement and evaluation.

One of the new aspects of the study was the list of Best Practices in Public Relations/Communication identified through statistical correlations. Here is the list of 13 Best Practices found:

1. Maintain a higher than average ratio of public relations budget to gross revenue (GAP/GR Ratio [Ratio of public relations Budget to Gross Revenue]).
2. Report directly and exclusively to the C-Suite.
3. Optimize the C-Suite's understanding of public relations' current and potential contributions to the success of the organization as a whole.
4. Establish an effective social responsibility strategy for your organization.
5. Establish an effective digital-media strategy for your organization.
6. Establish an effective issues-management strategy for your organization.
7. Optimize integration and coordination of Public Relations/Communications, both within the Public Relations/Communications function, and with other organizational functions.
8. Encourage highly ethical practices across the organization, beginning with communication.

9. Encourage the organization-wide adoption of a long-term strategic point of view, beginning with communication.

10. Encourage the organization-wide adoption of a proactive mindset, beginning with communication.

11. Encourage the organization-wide adoption of a flexible mindset, beginning with communication.

12. Optimize the integration of public relations and reputational considerations into top-level organizational strategies.

13. Measurably contribute to organizational success.

One of the most popular aspects of the study is the section on public relations budgeting as a percentage of revenue. The GAP Study refers to this as the public relations/GR Ratio. For this wave of the study, the ratio suggests that large organizations spend, on average, $786 on public relations for every $1 million in gross revenue. Those from smaller companies or agencies working with smaller clients should be advised that this ratio becomes nonsensical for smaller companies. The GAP V Study skews toward larger organizations. GAP V averages were gross revenue—$6.7B, public relations budget—$4.4 million and agency fees 30 percent of total public relations budget.

While the GAP V Study will have its critics, taken in proper context, it provides many useful data points that help add a little science to the art of public relations.

Let's Rein in the Hype About Relationship Measurement

(October 12, 2007)
There appears to be a groundswell of support among the measurement cognoscente (aka, metrosexuals) for the concept of *relationship measurement*. Much of the early work in relationship measurement was done by Dr. James Grunig and Dr. Linda Hon, as published in their seminal 1999 article: "Guidelines for Measuring Relationships in Public Relations." The basic premise of relationship measurement is that public relations is fundamentally about managing the relationship between an organization or company and all its stakeholders—employees, communities, customers,

partners, and so forth. Dr. Grunig and Dr. Hon identified six factors—
four characteristics of relationships and two types of relationships—that
collectively are highly correlated to relationship strength:

1. Control mutuality
2. Trust
3. Satisfaction
4. Commitment
5. Exchange relationship
6. Communal relationship

In my opinion, relationship measurement is an interesting concept
that has a place in the public relations measurement mix, primarily as a
diagnostic tool. It is not, however, a panacea nor should it be considered
the "next big thing" in measurement. Here's why:

- *With relationship measurement you are measuring the strategy
  (how) and not the objective (what).* A company wants better
  relationships with employees because that probably means
  their employee retention rates are higher, or their talent acqui-
  sition costs are lower, or perhaps because satisfied employees
  provide better customer service. They want better relationships with customers because they may buy more products or
  services and are more loyal. Relationships are the means to the
  end perhaps, but not the desired outcome.
- *There is no proof (yet) that better relationships lead directly to
  better business outcomes.* While it may be intuitively obvious to
  many of you that having better relationships is good for the
  business, the research necessary to demonstrate this has not
  been done in any broad-scale way of which I am aware.
- *It is difficult to demonstrate the value to the organization of public relations if we are focused on measuring relationships.* If you
  go into a CEO's office and he/she asks how public relations is
  doing this year and you respond, "Great, relationship strength
  is up an average of 12 percent across the board," you will get
  a very blank look in response. Like it or not, public relations

must demonstrate *how* it is helping to drive desired business outcomes if it is to be considered a core strategic function within the organization.

In the coming months I'm quite sure you will hear more and more about relationship measurement. Read the articles and the books. Experiment with it and see if it meets your needs. But please, can we keep a little perspective about what it is and what it is not? Thanks for reading. I welcome your contrary viewpoints.

(October 13, 2007)

Comments:

From **Katie Paine:**

Don, I have to take issue with you on a couple of points. First of all, in this social media age, all public relations is about relationships, whether it is relationships with the media, relationships with bloggers, or relationships with employees or your community. It's what we do—we manage and hopefully improve our relationships with all our various publics. That's why my book is called *Measuring Public Relationships* and why I provide specific measures for each public you're dealing with.

Secondly, there is lots of evidence that good relationships yield better outcomes. Read any number of the IPRRC (International Public Relations Research Conference) papers like Marcia Watson et al. who showed that good relationships result in lower legal costs and lower operating costs or Sandra Duhe who showed that good relationships with communities (CSR/corporate social responsibility) yielded higher overall financial outcomes.

(October 15, 2007)

From **Don Bartholomew:**

Greetings Katie,

Thanks for your thought-provoking comment—I would have been surprised only if you did not disagree with me on this issue. Let me address your second point first. I'll stand by my statement that there is no "broad-scale" proof or rigorous research that demonstrates the effects relationships have on business outcomes. Sure there are isolated studies, but I would suggest that there is not a sufficient body of work upon which to draw definitive conclusions.

Back to your first point. I am troubled by the statement, "all public relations is about relationships" (what about executive counsel, brand-building, crisis communications, and so forth?) because we are in a social media age. Social media is more about user-generated content and peer-to-peer communities than it is about relationships. We want to get consumers talking to each other about our companies, products, or services, not just facilitating a conversation between the consumer and the company. As you say in your own blog, Katie: it's more about engagement ("When more and more organizations are tying their communications activities to web traffic, donations and member sign ups and calculate ROI directly who cares how many eyeballs they reach? What really matters is the actions the target audience takes. Bye bye impressions, hello engagement."—Katie Paine). I believe that engagement and relationships are like the rectangle and the square—a relationship is engagement, but engagement is not necessarily a relationship.

In the social media age, rather than brands reaching out to communities (e.g., a target market), communities form around brands due to common interests and mutually beneficial interactions (e.g., you write a review of a product and I want to read it because I value your opinion).

I am also somewhat troubled by the premise that public relations professionals can somehow "manage" relationships. We sometimes facilitate them, but relationships essentially take on a life of their own without management by public relations professionals. Certainly within social media, individuals would resist being managed by an interested third party. Whether or not a relationship even exists is really up to the consumer—they get to decide if a relationship exists and what the boundaries and rules of the relationship are to be. This dynamic furthers complicates, and perhaps limits, the utility of relationship measurement in public relations.

(October 15, 2007)

From **Todd Defren:**

I agree with *both* of you.

I agree with Don that CEOs are unlikely to pat public relations on the back for "upping relationship strength by 12 percent" but also agree with Katie that better business outcomes are likely to result from good relationships.

I hate to quote a competitor but something Richard Edelman recently wrote has stuck with me: "Public Relations should stand for Public Relationships, a transparent effort to advocate our client's position, supported by depth of content, while offering an open place for dialogue and comment."

... Which to me means that public relations is morphing into a discipline that helps create and integrate "content"—makes it available to all interested parties—and then hosts, monitors, and participates in the ensuing conversations.

I am not sure how measurable this New World will be ... but I offer sincere kudos to bright minds like yours (Don and Katie) for trying to suss it all out.

(October 17, 2007)

From **Dr. James Grunig:**

Don,

Please allow me to make the case that priority should be given to measuring relationships in public relations. You are concerned on the value of relationships because you said (1) relationships measure a process or intermediate steps between public relations activities and "business outcomes," (2) relationships are not a "business outcome" valued by CEOs, and (3) there is no "proof" that relationships improve business outcomes.

First, you must realize that there are no universal business outcomes valued by all members of management and especially by all stakeholders. Organizational scholars discovered many years ago that organizations experience many competing objectives, depending on the perspective of different people working within the organization and different stakeholders outside the organization. Economists once thought that profit was the ultimate objective, but then they discovered that many people in the organization have different objectives. Sometimes growth is more important than profits for CEOs or investors. For marketing people, sales is probably the most important objective. For HR people, it might be employee productivity. For employees, income or career advancement is most important. Outside the organization, communities might value job creation, safety, or support for the community infrastructure. Environmental groups value low pollution. Government regulators value compliance with health and safety standards. We can go on and on.

In their book on the "stakeholder approach to management" (as opposed to the ownership approach), James Post, Lee Preston, and Sybille Sachs made a strong argument that different stakeholders value different performance objectives (business objectives in your terms) (Post, Preston, and Sachs 2002). Successful organizations produce the greatest value for all stakeholders when they develop relationships with the stakeholders that are most important for the organization (determined by how much the stakeholders affect the organization and how much the organization affects the stakeholders), developing performance objectives in collaboration with stakeholders, and then accomplishing these objectives. Therefore, you should be able to see that relationships are crucial both in identifying the most important performance objectives and then in accomplishing those objectives.

Second, relationships are more than a process objective. Accomplishing the performance objectives valued by all relevant stakeholders is the ultimate determinant of organizational effectiveness, but not all management functions contribute directly, or uniquely, to meeting those objectives. Before choosing an evaluation metric, it is important to conceptualize how and why the function we are evaluating (public relations) contributes to organizational effectiveness. Then we should choose a concept that captures what that function contributes that distinguishes it from other functions. The logic for choosing relationships as a focal measurement concept is the following: Public relations consists of communication activities designed to cultivate a relationship with the stakeholders that affect or are affected by organizational behaviors, policies, products, and services. Organizations that communicate symmetrically with publics are more likely to develop relationships high in trust, mutuality of control, satisfaction, and commitment than those who communicate asymmetrically or not at all. Organizations with good relationships with their stakeholders are more likely to choose performance objectives that are valued by those publics and are more likely to accomplish those objectives than those who have poor relationships. At the same time, there are many variables other than communication that contribute to the meeting of performance objectives. For example, sales are strongly affected by economic conditions, product quality, pricing, distribution, competition, quality of customer service, and so on. Communication makes a contribution, but to identify that contribution one must control for the effect of all the other variables.

We must understand how and why these variables interact to affect sales (or any other performance objective). The result is an extremely difficult, if not impossible, exercise in data gathering. Advocates of market mix modeling believe that they have controlled the data in this way, but I am not convinced that they have controlled for every relevant variable. I am especially not convinced that they can explain how public relations interacts with other variables to affect sales.

On the other hand, we can reason theoretically and find evidence to support our reasoning in basic research that explains why relationships are one of the most important variables performance objectives. Public relations is the organizational function responsible for relationships. It is not the primary function responsible for the other variables I mentioned. Therefore, we can measure the contribution of public relations most accurately by concentrating on what it does (cultivate relationships) and not concentrate on what it does not do (e.g., increase sales by itself). An accountant once told me that there are three ways to show the value of something: It can increase revenue, reduce cost, and reduce risk. Relationships do help to increase revenue, but if we concentrate only on revenue, we miss most of what public relations contributes by building relationships—reducing costs and risk. In choosing a metric, therefore, we often must step back from the final objective and measure the intermediary variable through which the function we are evaluating contributes to the final objective. I believe relationships are that variable.

It is also important to choose a metric that makes it possible to use research to improve what we do, not just to "prove" the value of what we are already doing. Many of my colleagues studying relationships have identified what we call *relationship cultivation strategies* (essentially a theoretical name for what public relations people do) that are most effective in affecting relationship outcomes (trust, mutuality of control, satisfaction, and commitment). If researchers measure both the type of cultivation strategies used as well as the relationship outcomes with which they are associated, they can gather important information that public relations professionals can use to improve their work.

Third, you said you do not believe that there is "proof" in the research literature that relationships are related to accomplishing performance objectives. It's important to understand that one never "proves" anything in science; that's a fundamental premise of the philosophy of science. What researchers do is gather evidence that supports their logical, theoretical explanations of how something works. The literature on public relations measurement is notoriously lacking in conceptualization—of explanations of how public relations works to accomplish organizational objectives. It's also important to recognize that one does not have to "prove" every component of a theory. It is sufficient to deduce likely indicators of an explanation to provide evidence to support it. Thus, it may be true that there are no studies that have measured a direct contribution of relationships to performance objectives. There are few studies that show the affect of any other management function in this way either—especially any that explain why there is such an effect. At the same time, the literature is filled with theories, research, and explanations that provide overwhelming evidence of the value of relationships in meeting performance objectives. You might start with chapter 3 of my book *Excellence in Public Relations and Communication Management* (Grunig 1992) and chapter 4 of its successor *Excellent Public Relations and Effective Organizations* (Grunig, Grunig, and Dozier 2002). The management literature on stakeholders (see the Post, Preston, and Sachs book mentioned earlier) (Post et al. 2002) and on reputation (such as the various books by Charles Fombrun) for additional evidence (e.g., Fombrun 1996; Fombrun and van Riel 2003).

Fourth, you said one cannot manage relationships. I agree. Relationships are an outcome of management or organizational decisions and behaviors. We can manage processes that, in turn, affect outcomes; but we cannot manage outcomes directly. We also cannot manage reputations, behaviors of others, images, perceptions, or many of the other outcomes used by public relations professionals to describe what they do. In public relations, we manage the communication behavior of organizations (both from publics to management and from management to publics), which in turn affect relationships. Relationships, along with many other variables, affect performance outcomes.

Finally, you said that public relations people use social media to get people to talk about your company or product. Perhaps. I believe, however, that people are much more likely to talk about a company or product if they have a relationship with it. And, I believe, others are more likely to pay attention to what people say about a company or product when those people have a relationship with it. For example, I recently bought a dehumidifier. My decision was heavily influenced by what people who owned each brand of dehumidifier said about it on the web.

(October 18, 2007)

From **Mark Weiner:**

Let me first identify myself as one of the marketing mix modeling advocates to whom Jim [Grunig] refers. Surprise Jim: I agree with you.

In May 2006, Jim and I had a published debate in IABC's (International Association of Business Communicators) *Communication World* in which Jim represented the merits of relationship-based public relations and I represented the merits of business results-based public relations (Communication World 2007).

Predicated on my experiences with dozens of marketing mix modeling cases, in which the use of sophisticated statistical modeling and advanced technology revealed a link between marketing and sales, which strongly favored public relations; public relations was found to deliver an average return of about $6.00 per dollar invested, mass-market advertising returned roughly $.20 on the dollar, price promotions lost $.25 on the dollar and so on ... public relations was tops not only because of its financial return but also because it provided a unique boost to other forms of marketing and enjoyed an extraordinarily slow decay rate.

But now that we've made the public relations-to-sales connection, what comes next? When one considers that public relations' decay rate can be as slow as six months before a campaign loses its ability to drive sales after the campaign ends (vs. advertising at two weeks and price promotions at less than 24 hours), one must ask "what is six months in the life of a brand?" The answer: "Not much."

I've come to realize that sales are a very important but fickle measure; the marketing may be spot-on but people are unreliable unless they are motivated to act differently. If you're like me, you price-shop; you compare; you buy whatever cereal is on sale because if it's sweet enough your kids will still eat it. What must brands do to preempt the capricious consumer? We must build a foundation of trust, engagement, differentiation, and clear value to earn the customer's loyalty: in a word, we must build "relationships" to drive successful, profitable, and enduring brands.

The debate between "relationships" and "business outcomes" is as moot as the age-old argument of the chicken-or-the-egg: who cares when you know you need both?

And sometimes, just sometimes, a dehumidifier is purchased not because of their marketing or your relationship with the manufacturer or its advocates: sometimes you simply have a wet basement.

Reflections on Relationship Measurement

(October 26, 2007)

The recent debate on relationship measurement in this blog (*more information in the article "Let's Rein in the Hype About Relationship Measurement" in Chapter 7*) was thought-provoking to me and I hope to you as well. I believe that there are at least three major areas of contention expressed or implied in the commentary:

Theory Versus Practice

One of the differences in opinion, I believe, may be attributed to the philosophic view that, "Public relations is the organizational function responsible for relationships" according to Dr. Grunig, and the practical reality of how public relations is currently viewed by professionals and the companies and agencies for whom they work. The practical reality is the public relations function today is rarely viewed as responsible for relationships in a broad organizational sense. The concept to me seems simultaneously too big and too limiting.

As a practical matter, marketing or brand managers or customer service/care executives are more often held responsible for customer relationships, not the public relations team. The responsibility for employee relationships more often lies in the human resources department than it does public relations. I could go on but you get the point. There is a large disconnect between the idealized organizational relationship model and the reality of the corporate world today.

Semantics

Many organizations today already perform various forms of research and measurement that might be categorized as relationship measurement. Three quick examples:

- *Voice of the Customer (VOC)* and variants are research techniques used to involve customers and prospects into the product or process design. A mechanism to have their voices heard before rather than after the fact.
- *Brand Studies* are regularly used to evaluate and measure the strength of the relationship between consumers and a product or company. Trust and emotional attachment are key concepts here.
- *Net Promoter Index* and other techniques used to assess the strength of relationships and satisfaction levels between customers and an organization.

Level of Abstraction

Building on the first topic, I would pose the question: do we want to stake the future of the public relations function on relationships? Is that our highest and best use within organizations? Clearly between media fragmentation and social media proliferation, the current focus of many professionals on media relations is a path akin to that formerly taken by the dinosaur. I believe the answer depends on the level of abstraction you want to apply. Three different levels come to mind:

- Relationships
- Influence
- Advocacy

A few thought leaders have organized their thinking around the concept of advocacy. Pragmatists might argue that the role of the profession is really about creating and facilitating influence—we create exposure and ultimately attempt to influence our constituents. Both of these concepts, to my way of thinking, are a higher level of abstraction than relationships. One might try to build relationships to increase influence. Or one might use relationship-building tactics to help create advocates for the brand or company.

The correct answer to this industry issue is clearly above my pay grade, but the debate is fascinating and important. Thanks for participating.

CHAPTER 8

Gaining Accountability— Making It Count

Don brought a very sophisticated capability to KGRA and helped us make sense of a media landscape that was (and is) really confusing. He pioneered two huge global social listening audits for a couple of our clients and helped us figure out how to do that on our own. Don's presence on the KGRA team made me feel good about the direction we were going. It made me feel safer and smarter just having him on the team because he was a true thought leader. He brought a lot of credibility to our group and helped launched our entire digital listening business. What I most loved about Don was that he gave us someone else to look up to.

—Lindsey Marshall, Vice President,
Research at Ketchum

This chapter includes:

- How to set measurement objectives appropriately
- How to determine the measurement orientation
- How to prove the value of the public relations profession
- How to make the results of public relations programs more accountable and have the public relations function gain a seat at the table

Left Brain Right for the Times

(April 6, 2006)

For years, the public relations profession has bemoaned the fact that it did not have a seat at the executive table. But in the post-Enron era, there is ample evidence—anecdotal and quantitative—that the communications function has finally climbed the hill. Here's just one data point—in a study of executives conducted by the American Advertising Federation (AAF) (Ries and Ries 2002), respondents were asked which departments were "Most Important" to their companies. Public Relations finished third, behind only Product Development and Strategic Planning, and ahead of powerful corporate functions such as R&D, Financial Strategies, Advertising, and Legal. Go ahead and gloat a little that an AAF study found Public Relations more important than Advertising.

Now that we have a seat at the table, we need to change our games to flourish in this environment. We believe there are three fundamental requirements:

1. Need to put public relations in the context of the business—demonstrate how public relations is helping to achieve corporate objectives.
2. Need to speak the language of the executive suite—and to some large degree that means quantification and metrics.
3. Need to be more accountable for results.

Let's pick up on the second point. The majority of public relations professionals are words people, not numbers guys; for most of us, the Right Brain rules. In the new environment, it will be increasingly important to get in touch with our Left Brains and enhance our comfort level with numbers, logic, and analysis. This is true in how we talk about public relations problems and opportunities, and as well as in the reporting of results. Consider this one simplified example. The CEO calls you in to ask your department to address an employee attitude issue that she believes is causing high levels of turnover. The traditional response may be to do a survey of employees to confirm the attitude issue, and then develop an employee communications program to improve attitudes. You then attempt to sell the program to the CEO based on past successes you have had in similar situations. In the new environment, you might still do the survey, but also supplement it with data about employee retention rates, costs to acquire new employees, and costs to train them properly. When you go back to the CEO, you are able to confirm the problem by saying:

Yes, we do have a problem, in fact, we estimate it is costing the company $3.1 million dollars per year. We believe this public relations program will impact about a third of this total, saving the company a little over one million dollars. This represents a ROI of over 300 percent.

Just think how much more powerful our position becomes (and how much greater our chances of getting budget approval) when we are able to quantify the problem in language that is comfortable to the CEO. Get in touch with your Left Brain.

Accountability No Longer Optional

(April 11, 2006)

In my last post, we discussed that one aspect of having a "seat at the table" is that the public relations function needs to be more accountable for results. While accountability may take several forms, at the most basic level it is about being responsible for one's actions and outcomes, that is, did you/your organization do what you said you would do? So how can we operationalize this concept in public relations?

We believe there are three fundamental opportunities for accountability across the public relations programming lifecycle:

1. *Quantify Opportunity/Problem*—At the time of assignment, the public relations team applies a little Left Brain thinking and quantifies the magnitude of the problem or opportunity that public relations will address. This was discussed in a previous post.
2. *Solution Quantification*—Once the programming is developed, but before it is approved and implemented, we should quantify the anticipated results for the program. This step answers the question, "If we accept this proposal/plan, what results or value might we reasonably expect?" It also sets up the third step ...
3. *Quantify Results*—The third stage of the framework occurs post-implementation and is the traditional measurement and evaluation phase.

The essence of accountability occurs when we compare the results we "promised" in stage 2 to the actual results measured in stage 3. The real kicker here is stage 2, which we may call "Solution Quantification." Public relations professionals have long been reluctant to predict in any specific way how much coverage, for example, will occur as a result of a given program or campaign. You may have heard this reluctance expressed as "public relations is an art, not a science." Regardless of the merits of this argument, we cannot use it as an excuse not to be accountable. Accountability is not easy. It is essential however if the public relations function is to maximize its potential impact on the organization.

Objective Failure

(April 17, 2006)

A baseline requirement for any successful public relations measurement program is to begin with *measurable objectives*. If the program objectives are not measurable, any effort to determine program success becomes subjective. The most common problem I have observed in all types of strategic plans during my career is poorly written objectives. So why is this so difficult? Two errors are common:

1. Writing objectives that are not specific enough with respect to metrics and timeframe to be measurable.
2. Confusing Objectives with Strategies.

An Objective is *What* you want to accomplish. It should have two essential elements—the specific target you hope to achieve and the time frame in which you plan to achieve it. Here are a couple of examples:

Poorly Constructed Objectives

- Increase awareness of product XYZ.
- Increase brand consideration for ABC.

Properly Written Objectives

- Increase awareness of Product XYZ from 15 to 25 percent in the next 12 months.

- Increase brand consideration for ABC from 45 to 75 percent by year-end 2007.

Generally, most people's Objectives are actually Strategies. They are *How* you hope to accomplish the goal, not *What* you ultimately wish to accomplish with the program. Sentences such as

- Position product XYZ as the technology leader in the segment
- Enhance visibility of brand ABC amongst 24 to 35 audience

would most likely be presented erroneously as Objectives, not Strategies. Here's an easy way to remember the difference:

- *Objective* What you want to accomplish
- *Strategy*   How you intend to achieve the Objective
- *Tactic*   Using or with what tools and techniques

It's free, easy, and absolutely necessary ... so why don't we do a better job of writing Objectives we can actually measure?

The Media Measurement Catch-22

(October 27, 2006)

"You Are What You Measure ..." I believe the first time I heard this phrase was from the mouth of Katie Delahaye Paine. I'm quite sure Katie didn't invent this phrase (it may have been Hauser and Katz in their excellent April 1998 article titled, "Metrics: You Are What You Measure!"), but I certainly have heard Katie use it repeatedly over the years we have known each other.

There is a corollary to this phrase that might go a little like this: If all you measure is media relations (primarily clip tonnage), that is how the public relations profession will be valued. I have heard or seen this from a number of measurement savvy people recently—Dr. Jim Grunig at the IPR Measurement Summit and Julia Hood in her October 2 column in *PRWeek* to name two. So the Catch-22 is this—while we all might agree that attempting to measure public relations is positive and to be encouraged, what we are measuring and how we are presenting the results is marginalizing our profession—clip book by clip book.

If public relations is to fully assume a seat at the executive table, we must address this Catch-22 in two fundamental ways:

1. We must do a better job of measuring and communicating all the value (tangible and intangible) delivered by public relations above and beyond media relations/clip counts—executive counsel, investor relations, employee communications, brand-building, reputation enhancement, crisis communications, …
2. We must connect the dots to show how public relations, including media relations, is helping to achieve desired business outcomes.

So, as Hauser and Katz (1998) suggest in their article, "Many metrics seem right and are easy to measure, but have subtle, counter-productive consequences." This is what I believe is happening today with our clip-happy mentality.

Hauser and Katz (1998) go on: "Other metrics are more difficult to measure, but focus the enterprise on those decisions and actions that are critical to success." Exactly!

Public Relations Residual Value

(November 28, 2007)

Did you ever have an idea and think that perhaps it is a "big idea?" You decide to sleep on it to see how it sounds in the cold light of morning. You wake up and realize, well this isn't really a big idea. In fact, maybe it's just a nice idea. Heaven forbid, some may even think it is a dumb idea! Your excitement of the prior evening has been replaced by a flood of doubt. That was my experience in thinking about a concept I'll call *Public Relations Residual Value* (PRrv).

The concept is simple enough. Public relations materials—releases, B-roll, product reviews, articles, blog postings, and so forth—have a value beyond the transactional value that occurs at the time of their appearance. By being archived on websites that are searchable, these materials have a shelf-life or longer-term value that transcends the shorter-term transactional value. The value is related to the degree to which the collection of public relations materials form a database that may be accessed by search engines such as Google, and the contribution the materials make toward search positioning on the specific search sites.

Various studies have shown that the majority of traditional journalists begin their story with a Google search. We also have ample anecdotal evidence that customers and consumers use search extensively to gather information and do comparative analysis of products and services. Clearly, having positive public relations materials among the top results for a given search has value, although it may be problematic to assign a specific value to this.

PRrv is certainly not a primary component of the value generated by public relations. But, if one is attempting to examine the total value generated by public relations—tangible and intangible, short term and longer term—then it may be worth considering.

Big, nice, or dumb idea is for you to decide. As always, your comments are very welcome and appreciated.

To Win Industry Awards Proper Measurement Is Crucial

(April 18, 2008)

I was honored this year to be asked by Paul Holmes to serve as a judge for the Sabre Awards. It was my first judging experience and I found it very rewarding and learned a lot. Across the five categories I judged there was a lot of great work by obviously talented professionals. With so much great work, it often comes down to which entry does the best job of demonstrating, through an effective measurement effort, stated objectives were met or exceeded. While there were good examples of this practice, there were many more submissions that simply failed to demonstrate the true success of their impressive campaigns.

Here are the three most common oversights of the nonwinning entries I reviewed:

- *Objectives Not Measurable*—The majority of the stated objectives in the entries, as written, were not measurable.

One cannot measure, "Increase Awareness" or "Generate Coverage." One could measure, "Increase Awareness from 10 to 25 percent in the Next 12 Months" or "Generate 1,000,000 Impressions in the First 6 Months of the Campaign."[1]

- *Strategies Masquerading as Objectives*—If objectives are "what" we want to accomplish, then strategies are "how." Sentences beginning with action words such as "leverage," "educate," "promote," or "communicate" are almost always a strategy and not an objective. Also, media coverage is almost always a strategy and not the objective. The vast majority of award entries had one or more strategies posing as objectives.

- *Measurement Misaligned with Objectives*—By misaligned I am referring to an objective that is an outcome (or influence) supported by measurement of only outputs (or exposure). If we are trying to create awareness or change an opinion, we cannot demonstrate success by only reporting on the number of impressions generated. Great programs articulate the desired business outcomes, write public relations objectives aligned with these outcomes, and then report on the metrics directly tied to the public relations objectives.

In summary, many of the entries made the hard stuff (great creativity and execution) look easy, and the easy stuff (writing proper objectives, measuring the correct metrics) look hard. Better than the other way around I guess. And lots of room for improvement.

---

[1] For more information, please refer to the following articles on "measurement objectives": "Social Media Metrics and Measurement Continue to Evolve" in Chapter 1; "Don't Let the Tool Tail Wag the Measurement Dog" in Chapter 4; "Let's Play 20 Questions: Social Media Measurement Style," "Three Fundamentals of Great Social Media Measurement," and "Social Media Measurement at a Crossroads" in Chapter 5; "AVEs Are a Disease—Here's a Little Vaccine" in Chapter 6; "Objective Failure" in Chapter 8.

Media Content Analysis: Are You Trying to Improve or Just Keeping Score?

(June 13, 2008)

One of the maddening aspects of working in public relations measurement is the emphasis on using the results to just keep score rather than using the data as a diagnostic tool to determine what is working and what is not. In other words, too much *What*, not enough *Why*. I have observed professionals involved with media analysis generally have an orientation toward one camp or the other. I'm not sure if one's measurement orientation is genetic or socialized but it is there.

Certainly the culture of the company or organization may reward one orientation over the other. In my experience many senior leaders of companies or organizations seem to reward scorekeeping over diagnostics. Perhaps this is natural for them, thinking someone else will worry about the Whys.

So how can you determine your measurement orientation? Here are a few statements to help guide you:

1. If the first question you ask when the quarterly measurement report arrives is, "How many hits did we get this month," you're a scorekeeper.

2. If you ask, "How many unique visitors to our blog did we get this month," you're just keeping score.

3. If you notice an explosion of positive comments about your brand in online forums and ask, "I wonder what is causing the explosion of positive comments, who is commenting, and how many are re-commenters," you are diagnostically oriented. A scorekeeper would immediately be most interested in the total number of comments and unique visitors.

4. If you are a huge advocate of indexing all public relations results to a single number on a 1–100 scale (a lá Microsoft and others), you are just keeping score.

5. If you are perfectly content with only measuring outputs, or Exposure as I prefer to say, and don't care so much about measuring outcomes (Influence), you most likely are a scorekeeper at heart.

There is a little scorekeeper in all of us. But, the highest and best use of media content analysis is as a diagnostic tool used to continually fine-tune and improve your public relations programs.

Two Keys to Low Cost Measurement

(July 23, 2008)

Cost is one of the key inhibitors of public relations measurement becoming more prevalent. It probably is *the* key inhibitor, with ignorance/lack of education a close second. Cracking the code on lowering total costs of measurement would go a long way toward making measurement the rule rather than the exception. In order to understand how to lower costs, you first have to understand *what* the largest cost drivers are in most measurement programs today. The primary cost drivers are content acquisition/aggregation and human analysis of articles.

Up to 40 percent of the total cost of a media content analysis program can simply be acquiring and aggregating the content to be measured. Common content services such as Factiva, Lexis Nexis, Bacons, eWatch, and VMS are not cheap. In order to cast a wide net, many public relations professionals feel that they need multiple services to cover (almost) every possible outlet where coverage may occur. Content costs can quickly get out of hand.

The other major cost driver is the need to have real humans analyze coverage. And no, automating article analysis is not a truly viable option right now. In my opinion, the accuracy of such systems is not high enough to justify the potential cost savings. Even with many content analysis operations being off-shored to low-cost countries such as India, the cost for analysis on a per article basis ranges from $1.50 to $3.00. If you are garnering a lot of coverage, these costs can add up in a hurry.

The good news is that one can address both these cost components by simply measuring a *subset* of your total coverage rather than every single article. There are two ways to accomplish this—by taking an nth sample of your total coverage, or, the approach I prefer, determining the relatively short list of publications/outlets that have the most influence on your targets and only measuring coverage within this smaller population. By relatively short, think 100 total publications or less. With a little work, you can probably get your list down to 50 outlets that really make a difference. I worked with a Fortune 500 company that targeted 64 publications they felt really helped move their business. That is 64 *globally*.

By confining your measurement program to the most important and influential outlets, you hold down both content and analysis costs. So why don't more people pursue this easy fix? I believe it goes back to the industry attitude that views measurement as a scorekeeping mechanism more so than a diagnostic tool. If our industry remains prisoners of the "tonnage" model of coverage, then measurement cost reduction is very difficult.

To conclude on a positive note, the quality of the free content sources and tools is getting better and better. Now that it supports archiving, Google News is a viable source to acquire content. Google Analytics and BlogPulse from Nielsen Buzzmetrics provide some interesting blog and website metrics at an aggressive price point—free.

Is 2009 the Tipping Point for Social Media Accountability?

(November 5, 2008)

Social media use and measurement to date has mostly resided in the experimentation stage. In the last couple of years there has been a rush to experiment and become involved with the exciting new world of digital and social media. Press conferences in Second Life. Posting corporate podcasts on YouTube. Not relying on others to publish your company content—just publish it yourself.

All of this comes with a price tag. So far, the spirit of experimentation has provided a sort of "get out of jail free" card with respect to having to demonstrate the value of digital and social media programs and initiatives. It looks like the year 2009 will change all that due primarily to three factors:

- the widespread awareness of social media use in a business context;
- the economy; and
- the economy.

The year 2009 will raise the bar on all of us to demonstrate how social media programs are helping to drive desired business outcomes. It won't be enough to just report on the number of view-throughs for a clip or unique commenters on a blog. We will be challenged to explain how our programs will drive consumer/customer awareness, engagement, and purchase intent. How we are contributing to the brand and how does the contribution impact the business. The questions will outnumber our answers, but we all better be ready to come up with better answers than we have in the past. The year 2009 will be the year when the pendulum swings from experimentation to accountability. Buckle your seat belts.

Capturing the Total Value of Public Relations

(December 15, 2008)

Since public relations is a broad profession and may cover a wide variety of disciplines—media relations, online engagement, crisis communications, public affairs, executive counseling, brand-building, events, reputation management, employee communications, and financial communications, to name a few—it is difficult to conceptualize the totality of value public relations and communication delivers to the organization. For the most part, public relations measurement has focused on attempts to measure media relations value and is not really addressing the other areas very well. When you are attempting to quantify the full value and ROI of public relations, taking the broad view paints a much richer picture.

The public relations *Value Cube* is a tops-down conceptual framework for capturing all the ways public relations is contributing value to the organization. Public relations contributes value in one of these three major, interrelated areas (Y-axis):

- *Marketing*—Sales and other marketing-oriented programs and metrics (e.g., lead generation) fit within this category. The vast majority of public relations measurement efforts today fall within the Marketing category.
- *Brand*—Public relations contributes to building brands. Value contribution in this area is usually more anecdotal

than measured. Experiential public relations and many social media campaigns are contributing more to brand than sales or any other area.

- *Reputation*—One of the primary overarching purposes of public relations is reputation enhancement and protection, yet our contribution here again is usually measured more by "gut metrics" than analytics.

Within each major area we can examine through Figure 8.1 value created through Engagement, Influence, and Action (X-axis).

- *Engagement*—To what degree has exposure to public relations materials, activities, and events created Engagement with the intended target audience? Are they interacting with our content, creating links, forwarding to friends, talking about the brand, and so forth?
- *Influence*—The degree to which Engagement has influenced perceptions and attitudes. Likelihood to recommend the brand to a friend and brand consideration changes are two possible examples of Influence.
- *Action*—As a result of the public relations effort, what actions if any has the target taken? Did they visit the website, tell a friend, buy the product, vote for our candidate, and so forth?

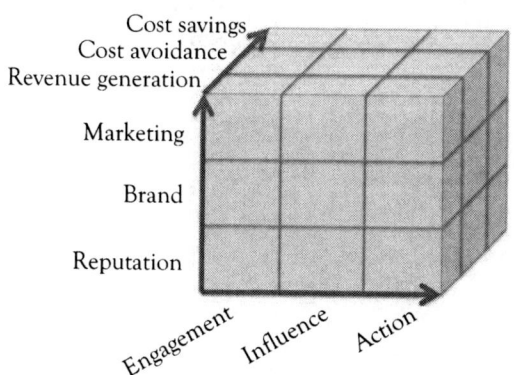

Figure 8.1 Public relations value cube

The value itself can take one of three forms (Z-axis):

- *Revenue generation*
- *Cost savings* (e.g., employee recruiting costs decline due to strong company reputation)
- *Cost avoidance* (e.g., avoiding recruiting costs because employee retention/loyalty has improved)

There is one more important consideration when thinking about the total value delivered by public relations and social media. That is time. Public relations creates value on a transactional, short-term basis (e.g., the value of 10,000 potential customers reading your article in today's *Wall Street Journal*) and on a process-oriented, longer-term basis. Brand and Reputation are both examples of longer-term value. Both are process-oriented, and build and lose value over time, often measured in years. The other time dimension value created by public relations is what I have referred to previously as the *residual value of public relations*. That is the value of the created searchable and archived content created by the public relations function. The residual value may take the form of influencing organic search positioning.

That's a lot of value for one profession! In 2009, let's hope CEOs, CMOs, and other decision-makers increasingly recognize the great value and superior ROI delivered by public relations.

References

Adams, R. 2006. "The Story that Stats Don't Tell: Number Crunchers, a Big Hit in Baseball, Have Had Less-Stellar Results in the NBA." *The Wall Street Journal*, April 15. www.wsj.com/articles/SB114504083095226278 (accessed March 11, 2016).

AMEC (International Association for the Measurement and Evaluation of Communication). 2013a. "Unlocking Business Performance: Communications Research and Analytics in Action." http://amecorg.com/wp-content/uploads/2013/06/Social-Media-Valid-Framework2013.pdf (accessed March 11, 2016).

AMEC (International Association for the Measurement and Evaluation of Communication). 2013b. "European Summit Success." http://amecorg.com/2013/06/european-summit-success/ (accessed March 11, 2016).

Balanced Scorecard Institute. 2009. "The Balanced Scorecard and Its Relationship to Operations Management." www.asq509.org/ht/a/GetDocumentAction/id/45098 (accessed March 11, 2016).

Bialik, C. 2011. "Publicists Pump Up Value of Buzz; Don't Believe the Hype." *The Wall Street Journal*, June 25. www.wsj.com/articles/SB10001424052702303339904576405683745990342 (accessed March 11, 2016).

Burke, S. 2015. "In Memoriam: Don Bartholomew, Godfather of the Measurati," *Shonali Burke Consulting, Inc.* http://shonaliburke.com/2015/06/05/in-memoriam-don-bartholomew-godfather-of-the-measurati/ (accessed March 11, 2016).

BurrellesLuce. 2008. "Copyright Compliance: How to Legally Share Newsclips." www.burrellesluce.com/resources/newsletter/2008/february_2008 (accessed March 11, 2016).

Cha, M., H. Haddadi, F. Benevenuto, and K.P. Gummadi. 2010. "Measuring User Influence in Twitter: The Million Follower Fallacy." *Association for the Advancement of Artificial Intelligence.* http://twitter.mpi-sws.org/icwsm2010_fallacy.pdf (accessed March 11, 2016).

Chen, S. March 19, 2009. "Newspapers Fold as Readers Defect and Economy Sours." *CNN.* www.cnn.com/2009/US/03/19/newspaper.decline.layoff/index.html (accessed March 11, 2016)

Communication World. May–June 2007. "The Public Relations Debate: Two Leaders in the Profession Discuss What PR Is, How It Works and Where It's Going." *Communication World* 24, no. 3, pp. 26+.

Corcoran, S. 2011. "Introducing 'Social Maturity': How Social Media Transforms Companies," *Forrester*. http://blogs.forrester.com/sean_corcoran/11-06-02-introducing_social_maturity_how_social_media_transforms_companies (accessed March 11, 2016).

Court, D., D. Elzinga, S. Mulder, and O.J. Vetvik. June 2009. "The Consumer Decision Journey." *McKinsey Quarterly*. www.mckinsey.com/business-functions/marketing-and-sales/our-insights/the-consumer-decision-journey (accessed March 11, 2016).

Defren, T. 2009. "Audience Targeting on Social Media." *PR Squared* www.pr-squared.com/index.php/2009/05/audience-targeting-in-social-media (accessed March 11, 2016).

Edelman. 2009. "2009 Edelman Trust Barometer Executive Summary." www.edelman.com/assets/uploads/2014/01/2009-Trust-Barometer-Executive-Summary.pdf (accessed March 11, 2016).

Edelman. 2015. "2015 Edelman Trust Barometer." www.edelman.com/insights/intellectual-property/2015-edelman-trust-barometer/ (accessed March 11, 2016).

Edwards, J. March 27, 2013. "What Is a Facebook 'Like' Actually Worth in Dollars?" *Business Insider*. www.businessinsider.com/what-is-a-facebook-like-actually-worth-in-dollars-2013-3 (accessed March 11, 2016).

e-Marketer. 2009. "Social Media Measurement Lags Adoption: ROI Metrics Neglected by Most." www.emarketer.com/Article/Social-Media-Measurement-Lags-Adoption/1007286 (accessed March 11, 2016).

Fombrun, C.J. 1996. *Reputation: Realizing Value from the Corporate Image*. Boston, MA: Harvard Business School Press.

Fombrun, C.J., and C.B.M. van Riel. 2003. *Fame & Fortune: How Successful Companies Build Winning Reputations*. Upper Saddle River, NJ: Financial Times Prentice Hall.

Forrester Research. n.d. "The Customer Life-Cycle Marketing Playbook." www.forrester.com/The+Customer+LifeCycle+Marketing+Playbook/-/E-PLA660 (accessed March 11, 2016).

Grunig, J.E. 1992. *Excellence in Public Relations and Communication Management*. New York: Routledge.

Grunig, L.A., Grunig, J.E., and D. Dozier. 2002. *Excellent Public Relations and Effective Organizations: A Study of Communication Management in Three Countries*. Mahwah, NJ: Lawrence Erlbaum Associates.

Hauser, J.R., and G.M. Katz. 1998. "Metrics: You Are What You Measure!" *Massachusetts Institute of Technology*. www.mit.edu/~hauser/Papers/Hauser-Katz%20Measure%2004-98.pdf (accessed March 11, 2016).

Hon, L.C., and J.E. Grunig. 1999. "Guidelines for Measuring Relationships in Public Relations." *Institute for Public Relations*. www.instituteforpr.org/

wp-content/uploads/Guidelines_Measuring_Relationships.pdf (accessed March 11, 2016).

Institute for Public Relations. 2010. "The Barcelona Declaration of Research Principles." www.instituteforpr.org/the-barcelona-declaration-of-research-principles/ (accessed March 11, 2016).

Institute for Public Relations. 2011. "Public Relations Industry Sets Top Four Measurement Priorities." www.instituteforpr.org/public-relations-industry-sets-top-four-measurement-priorities/ (accessed March 11, 2016).

Institute for Public Relations. 2015. "Barcelona Principles 2.0—Updated 2015." www.instituteforpr.org/barcelona-principles-2-0-updated-2015/ (accessed March 11, 2016).

Krotoski, A. 2010. "Robin Dunbar: We Can Only Ever Have 150 Friends at Most …" *The Guardian*, March 13. www.theguardian.com/technology/2010/mar/14/my-bright-idea-robin-dunbar (accessed March 11, 2016).

Lionbridge. 2013. "What Are Double-Byte, Single-Byte, and Multi-Byte Encodings?" http://info.lionbridge.com/rs/lionbridge/images/Lionbridge%20FAQ_encoding_2013.pdf?utm_source=blog&utm_medium=copy&utm_campaign=encoding+blog (accessed March 11, 2016).

Michaelson, D., and D.W. Stacks. 2007. "Exploring the Comparative Communications Effectiveness of Advertising and Public Relations: An Experimental Study of Initial Branding Advantage." *Institute for Public Relations*. www.instituteforpr.org/wp-content/uploads/Michaelson_Stacks.pdf (accessed March 11, 2016).

Miller, C. 2009. "Spinning the Web: P.R. in Silicon Valley." *The New York Times*, July 4. www.nytimes.com/2009/07/05/business/05pr.html?_r=3&th&emc=th& (accessed March 11, 2016).

Moran, F. 2009. "Social Media Adoption yet to Cross the Chasm—IDC." *Francis Moran & Associates*. http://francis-moran.com/marketing-strategy/social-media-adoption-yet-to-cross-the-chasm-idc/ (accessed March 11, 2016).

Neff, J. 2009. "Study: ROI May be Measurable in Facebook, MySpace After All: Package-Goods Brand Earns $1.28 Million in Sales From $1 Million Social-Media Campaign." *AdAge*. http://adage.com/article/digital/study-cpg-roi-measurable-facebook-myspace/135940/ (accessed March 11, 2016).

Nielsen. n.d. "Nielsen BuzzMetrics®: The Global Measurement Standard in Consumer-Generated Media." www.nielsen.com/content/dam/nielsen/en_us/documents/pdf/Fact%20Sheets/Nielsen%20BuzzMetrics%20Fact%20Sheet.pdf (accessed March 11, 2016).

Paine, K.D. 2012. "Who Are the Measurati that Are Setting Social Media Measurement Standards?" *The Measurement Standard: Blog Edition*. http://kdpaine.blogs.com/themeasurementstandard/2012/05/who-are-the-measurati-that-are-setting-social-media-measurement-standards.html (accessed March 11, 2016).

Peterson, E.T. 2006. "How Do You Calculate Engagement? Part I." http://analyticsdemystified.com/adobe-analytics/how-do-you-calculate-engagement-part-i/ (accessed March 11, 2016).

Post, J., L.E. Preston, and S. Sachs. 2002. *Redefining the Corporation: Stakeholder Management and Organizational Wealth*. Redwood City, CA: Stanford University Press.

Ries, A., and L. Ries. 2002. *The Fall of Advertising and the Rise of PR*. New York: HarperCollins.

Rockland, D. 2011. "PR Measurement Beyond the Barcelona Principles." *Ragan's PR Daily*. www.prdaily.com/Main/Articles/PR_measurement_beyond_the_Barcelona_Principles_9263.aspx (accessed March 11, 2016).

Sheldrake, P. 2011. *The Business of Influence: Reframing Marketing and PR for the Digital Age*. Hoboken, NJ: John Wiley & Sons.

Sheldrake, P. 2013. "Social Media Measurement, After Madrid." www.philipsheldrake.com/2013/06/social-media-measurement-after-madrid/ (accessed March 11, 2016).

Soares, S. 2012. "Big Data Governance: A Framework to Assess Maturity." *IBM Big Data & Analytics Hub*. www.ibmbigdatahub.com/blog/big-data-governance-framework-assess-maturity (accessed March 11, 2016).

Solis, B. 2008. "Twitter Tools for Marketing and Community Professionals." *Brian Solis*. www.briansolis.com/2008/10/twitter-tools-for-community-and/ (accessed March 11, 2016).

Solis, B. 2009. "PR Does Not Stand for Press Release: Equalizing Spikes and Valleys." *Brian Solis*. www.briansolis.com/2009/07/pr-does-not-stand-for-press-release-equalizing-spikes-and-valleys/ (accessed March 11, 2016).

Stacks, D.W., and S.A. Bowen. 2013. *The Dictionary of Public Relations Measurement and Research*. 3rd ed. Institute for Public Relations. www.instituteforpr.org/dictionary-public-relations-measurement-research-third-edition/ (accessed March 11, 2016).

Swerling, J., J. Gregory, J. Schuh, T. Goff, J. Gould, X. Gu, K. Palmer, and A. Mchargue. 2007. "Fifth Annual Public Relations Generally Accepted Practices (G.A.P.) Study (2007 Data)." *USC Annenberg Strategic Public Relations Center*. http://annenberg.usc.edu/ResearchCenters/The%20USC%20Center%20for%20Public%20Relations/~/media/B63DF36350EA44748B1DFEA6F4913ACD.ashx (accessed March 11, 2016).

Swerling, J., I. Mitroff, J. Hall, D. King, L. Benson, and P. O'Boyle. 2005. "Fourth Annual Public Relations Generally Accepted Practices (G.A.P.) Study (2005 Data)." *USC Annenberg Strategic Public Relations Center*. http://annenberg.usc.edu/ResearchCenters/The%20USC%20Center%20for%20Public%20Relations/~/media/9D8F5F00364749E8B31FE47B77FEFF0C.ashx (accessed March 11, 2016).

The Conclave Social Media Measurement Standards. 2013. "The Conclave Complete Social Media Measurement Standards June 2013." www.smmstandards.com/wp-content/uploads/2013/06/Complete-standards-document4.pdf (accessed March 11, 2016).

The Conclave Social Media Measurement Standards. n.d. "The Standards—2. Reach and Impression." http://smmstandards.wix.com/smmstandards#!reach-and-impressions/c1g4r (accessed March 11, 2016).

The Measurement Standard. 2015. "Tributes to Don Bartholomew, Godfather of the Measurati." www.themeasurementstandard.com/2015/06/tributes-to-don-bartholomew-godfather-of-the-measurati/ (accessed March 11, 2016).

Weiner, M., and D. Bartholomew. 2006. "Dispelling the Myth of PR Multipliers and Other Inflationary Audience Measures." *Institute for Public Relations.* www.instituteforpr.org/dispelling-myth-pr-multipliers/ (accessed March 11, 2016).

Zavarello, M. 2010. "New Metrics Are No Excuse to Continue a Pattern of Lazy Analytics: An Example Using Klout." *Bright Matrices.* http://blog.bright-matrix.net/2010/08/30/new-metrics-are-no-excuse-to-continue-a-pattern-of-lazy-analytics-an-example-using-klout/ (accessed March 11, 2016).

Index

OTHER TITLES IN OUR PUBLIC RELATIONS COLLECTION

Don W. Stacks and Donald K. Wright, Editors

- *A Professional and Practitioner's Guide to Public Relations Research, Measurement, and Evaluation, Second Edition* by David Michaelson and Donald W. Stacks
- *Leadership Communication: How Leaders Communicate and How Communicators Lead in Today's Global Enterprise* by E. Bruce Harrison and Judith Muhlberg
- *The Public Relations Firm* by Stacey Smith and Bob Pritchard
- *The Social Media Communication Matrix: A New Direction in Public Relations* by Kenneth D. Plowman and Beki Winchel
- *Public Relations Ethics: How To Practice PR Without Losing Your Soul* by Dick Martin and Donald K. Wright

Business Expert Press has over 30 collection in business subjects such as finance, marketing strategy, sustainability, public relations, economics, accounting, corporate communications, and many others. For more information about all our collections, please visit www.businessexpertpress.com/collections.

Business Expert Press is actively seeking collection editors as well as authors. For more information about becoming an BEP author or collection editor, please visit http://www.businessexpertpress.com/author

Announcing the Business Expert Press Digital Library

Concise e-books business students need for classroom and research

This book can also be purchased in an e-book collection by your library as

- a one-time purchase,
- that is owned forever,
- allows for simultaneous readers,
- has no restrictions on printing, and
- can be downloaded as PDFs from within the library community.

Our digital library collections are a great solution to beat the rising cost of textbooks. E-books can be loaded into their course management systems or onto students' e-book readers. The **Business Expert Press** digital libraries are very affordable, with no obligation to buy in future years. For more information, please visit **www.businessexpertpress.com/librarians**. To set up a trial in the United States, please email **sales@businessexpertpress.com**.

CPSIA information can be obtained
at www.ICGtesting.com
Printed in the USA
FFOW02n1055260816
26986FF